The Road to Romance + Ruin

TEEN FILMS AND YOUTH CULTURE

JON LEWIS

WITHDRAWN

ROUTLEDGE
NEW YORK • LONDON

 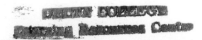

PN
1995.9
.Y6
L49
1992

Published in 1992 by

Routledge
An imprint of Routledge, Chapman and Hall, Inc.
29 West 35th Street
New York, NY 10001

Published in Great Britain by

Routledge
11 New Fetter Lane
London EC4P 4EE

Copyright © 1992 by Routledge, Chapman and Hall, Inc.

Printed in the United States of America

All rights reserved. No part of this book may be reprinted or reproduced or utilized in any form or by any electronic, mechanical or other means, now known or hereafter invented, including photocopying and recording, or in any information storage or retrieval system, without permission in writing from the publisher.

Library of Congress Cataloging-in-Publication Data

Lewis, Jon, 1955–
    The road to romance and ruin : teen films and youth culture / Jon Lewis.
        p.   cm.
    Includes bibliographical references.
    ISBN 0-415-90426-9 — ISBN 0-415-90427-7 (pbk.)
    1. Youth in motion pictures. 2. Authority in motion pictures.
    3. Motion pictures—Plots, themes, etc.   I. Title.
PN1995.9.Y6L49   1992
791.43'655—dc20   92-3311
                                                                     CIP

British Library Cataloguing in Publication Data

Lewis, Jon
    Road to Romance and Ruin: Teen Films and Youth Culture
    I. Title
    791.43
    ISBN 0-415-90426-9 hb
    ISBN 0-415-90427-7 pbk

WITHDRAWN

with big love etc.
for Q. and Guy Monroe

Contents

Acknowledgments

Many thanks to Dana Polan and Eric Patterson, Robert Self, my parents, the Oregon Committee for the Humanities, the Center for the Humanities at Oregon State University, and (on the home front) Martha and Mocha J.

Introduction

By my best estimate, my daughter was two or three thousand years old when she was born. She never manifested any discernable interest in sex, drugs, rock 'n' roll, cars, dresses, or the stock market. She used a $65,000 Vassar education to learn how to become a Tibetan Buddhist nun specializing in carpentry.[1]

Life is sheer ambiguity. If a person doesn't see this, he's either an asshole or a fascist.[2]

By some time in the mid-1990s over half the earth's population will be under the age of twenty.[3] For better or worse, the world is getting younger.

At this writing, there are 1.37 billion teenagers on the planet.[4] And though it is a source of some dismay for the shrinking majority, "youth" is rapidly becoming the "dominant," the "official" culture. That we now need to take "them" seriously seems hardly worth arguing anymore.

But what is it that comprises "their" culture? Do "they" even have a "culture"? And how can we begin to talk about it?

Teen Films and Youth Culture

Youth is fragmentary and fleeting, transitional and transitory. Of late, as the academy has warmed to the importance (if not the merits) of the popular and the proletarian, youth culture has become the focus of considerable critical interest. But while much of the recent work is compelling, youth culture has proven to be an elusive target.

1

In the pages that follow I will present several potential interventions, several potential avenues into the serious study of youth culture. It is well worth noting, by way of introduction, that I am not a teenager. I write from a considerable critical distance. My principal objective claim is that the study of youth is by necessity inexact and incomplete. With teenagers, we must always be flexible.

Of primary interest to this study will be the teen film, seen here as the principal mass mediated discourse of youth; a discourse that rather glibly and globally re-presents youth as a culture. My definition of the teen film is at once obvious and unusual. Put simply, I plan to study films about teenagers, not films targeted at teenagers. The latter category includes the vast majority of the mainstream product now that the industry has embraced the adolescent as its ideal audience. A book about teen-targeted films would go a long way towards providing an understanding of the "new Hollywood." But, alas, this is not that book.

Genre, as it is used here, begins with the text, not with industry intent or with target audiences. Nevertheless, the teen films I discuss here do assemble a youth(ful) audience. But as opposed to the multitude of films targeted at teens, the movie about teenagers engages a unique dynamic. These teen films bring global youth and its (American) mirror/screen image face to face. For teenagers all over the planet, the effect is at once complex and contradictory; a mixture of desire and dread, irony and self-loathing.

In the pages that follow, I will attend to how teen films narrativize—how they give order to—the otherwise chaotic and contradictory experience of youth. These narratives historicize youth, contextualize youth, re-contextualize youth, re-present youth. Narrative is seen here as inherently ideological, inherently social—an authorizing force in a culture that is at once systematically ridiculed and idealized by those unlucky of us on the outside looking in.

Of specific interest here is how youth culture and the films that represent it speak to the central issues of post-World War II society, for example: the baby boom; the shifting of vast, homogeneous groups of the population; the sexual revolution; and the exponential expansion of the mass media. Youth's resort to anomie, deviance, promiscuity and sexual experimentation, conspicuous consumption, rebellion and regression—a list of "options" corresponding to the six

chapters that follow—finds global expression in American (and to a lesser extent, British) teen movies and in these films' corollary narratives, teen novels and rock and roll music.

Of central importance to this text is the argument that despite stylistic, tonal, industrial, and by now even generational differences within the genre, teen films all seem to focus on a single social concern: the breakdown of traditional forms of authority: patriarchy; law and order; and institutions like the school, the church, and the family. But while sociologists argue that the rapid succession of youth subcultures since the Second World War seem to have rejected the convention of authority *tout court,* the teen film has rather enthusiastically negotiated the reverse. By and large, the teen film presides over the eventual discovery of viable and often traditional forms of authority (for example: patriarchy at the end of *Rebel Without a Cause* [Nicholas Ray, 1955], law and order at the end of *The Wild One* [Laslo Benedeck, 1954], the charismatic elite at the end of *Heathers* [Michael Lehmann, 1989])—in effect, the restoration of the adult culture informed rather than radicalized by youth.

The astonishing emergence of youth culture after the Second World War (as a distinct, moneyed, seemingly homogeneous subculture with its own set of rituals and practices) prompted an immediate response from the burgeoning postwar consumer-leisure industry. Just as sociologists and cultural historians began talking about the phenomenon of youth culture, the advertising, recording, television, and movie industries took aim at this new target market. Today, in order to study youth culture adequately, we must focus on the essential paradox of youth as both mass movement and mass market.

Such a paradox characterizes the production and reception of the teen film—works that provide youth with a wealth of substantive images and re-presentation(s) of their lives that to a large extent originate from outside the teen experience. These films provide at best the principal artifacts of youth culture; at worst, they offer proof positive of the hegemonic effect of "the culture industry" (the argument that the media not only produce texts for consumption, but ideology for consumption as well; the argument that culture is yet another product of postwar industry). Given such a dialectic, one cannot study culture without attending to the re-presentations of that culture in the media.

3

The Culture is the Commodity/The Commodity is the Culture

When we are talking about youth, we are talking about a fundamentally mediated culture, one that continues to re-present itself in terms of the products it buys, the art that defines it, and the art it defines as its own. This dialectic of cultural autonomy and media appropriation—the paradox of a media-made culture and a culture that makes media—resides at the heart of a by now half-century-old debate, one that has dominated the study of youth just as it will dominate this study.

At one pole in this debate we find the Frankfurt School model and Theodor Adorno's concept of culture as a standard of excellence, as the best a society has to offer, as that which is not consumed or readily understood by the masses. Adorno, who coined the term "the culture industry," saw youth culture as the logical product of postwar media, derisively characterizing "the gesture of adolescence" as that "which raves for this or that on one day with the ever-present possibility of damning it as idiocy the next."[5] In a particularly colorful and apt turn of a phrase, Adorno quips that, in mass (youth) culture, "conformity replace(s) consciousness,"[6] that culture is systematically eroded by media that engender "a pleasure (in) a particular kind of consumption (and a) passive, endlessly repeated confirmation of the world as it is."[7] According to Adorno, as we study contemporary society, we end up talking less about culture than about the media, less about genius and achievement and more about the masses' descent into chaos, powerlessness, and privation.

Such a view of commodity culture—such a view of the culture of the commodity—is updated in Guy Debord's icy monologue *Society of the Spectacle*. For Debord, Adorno's dire prophecy has come to pass; the economic has supplanted the social, and human endeavor has been sundered to "the obvious degradation of *being* into *having*."[8] The media engage "a concrete manufacture of alienation,"[9] Debord argues, a separation from power and happiness in the very formation of culture, the very formation of a society made to cohere in terms of mass-mediated stereotypes, narratives, and slogans.

Adorno and Debord refuse to see commodity culture as a two-way street; in other words they refuse to see any active set of choices

4

exerted in the act of consuming conspicuously. For Adorno, youth's happy mindlessness and passive consumption characterize a pervasive erosion of standards, a "masochistic adjustment to authoritarian collectivism."[10] For Debord, consumption results in "generalized autism," an "imprisonment in a flattened universe . . . know(ing) only the *fictional speakers* who unilaterally surround (us) with their commodities and the politics of their commodities."[11]

An alternative to the culture-industry model emerged in the United States in the 1960's. Erik Erikson, Bruno Bettleheim, S. N. Eisenstadt, Talcott Parsons, Reuel Denney and Kenneth Keniston outlined a "psycho-social"/Oedipal model and posed the controversial argument that youth's growing dysfunction was the direct result of the failure of the adult society. Erikson et al. cite as causes for dysfunctional, deviant youth such phenomena as the breakdown of traditional forms of authority and social regulation; the absence of widely acknowledged rites of passage into adulthood; and the adult generation's inability to re-present their own culture as inviting, interesting, or even worth living.

Youth, Erikson quips, is characterized in terms of its difference from "a standard human being . . . judged on the basis of what it is not and will never be, or is not quite yet, or is not any more."[13] For Erikson et al., youth is viewed as a symptom, an emblem, a sign that something has gone terribly wrong in the culture at large.

Such a critical posit is recontextualized with regard to the culture/media dichotomy in Dick Hebdige's influential contemporary sociological study of youth, *Subculture: The Meaning of Style.* For Hebdige, youth's appropriation of and to an extent its appropriation by material culture reveals a dramatic "refusal," a stylized repudiation of adult culture that "in spectacular fashion (signals) the breakdown in consensus in the post-war period."[14] In its rituals and practices, its spectacular style, youth engages an ongoing cycle of resistance and defusion, autonomy and incorporation, diversity and fidelity, exile and assimilation.[15] Though he never refers specifically to Erikson et al., Hebdige attends to "the challenge of youth" with much the same premise regarding cultural deviance. But while the "psycho-social" American school searches for a cure, Hebdige rather celebrates the "disease." For Hebdige, chaos is inherently revolutionary, instinctively progressive.

5

Though he is cognizant of the media's role in culture, Hebdige departs from the Frankfurt School approach. Indeed, Hebdige seems to view youth as the era's last great proletariat. But such a romantic notion reveals more enthusiasm than reason, and even Hebdige is led to conclude that "cultures of resistance sometimes serve to reinforce rather than erode existing social structures."[16] In the final analysis, the very act of refusal is hegemonic.

Youth's "use" of the commodity in its own fluctuating self-image problematizes the concept of cultural autonomy. With that in mind, Stuart Hall poses the following flexible definition of culture: "As social groups and classes live, if not in their productive then in their social relations, increasingly fragmented and sectionally differentiated lives, the mass media are more and more responsible (a) for providing the basis on which groups and classes construct an image of the lives, meanings, practices and values of other groups and classes; (b) for providing the images, representations and ideas around which the social totality comprised of all these separate and fragmented pieces can be grasped."[17] In Hall's model, the media "situate resistance within the dominant order," effectively incorporating youth within "the dominant mythology from which it in part emanates."[18] It should not surprise us then, Hall concludes, "that much of what finds itself encoded in subculture has already been subjected to a certain amount of prior handling by the media."[19]

In *Sound Effects: Youth, Leisure and the Politics of Rock 'n' Roll*, Simon Frith attempts to unpack the contradictions inherent in youth's commodity-oriented culture. First, he characterizes the American school, and in doing so dismisses it as apolitical and overly psychological. "The young become a social problem only when they refuse to grow up," Frith posits, "and the refusal to grow up (this was a common sociological theme in the 1960's) is not a political act but an Oedipal one."[20] In the process of setting up his approach, Frith alludes to Hall and Paddy Whannel's definition of mass culture as "a contradictory mixture of the authentic and manufactured—an area for self-expression for the young and lush grazing ground for the commercial producers."[21] Indeed, Frith echoes Hall and Whannel when he notes that "the fact that young people are heavily involved in commercial institutions does not mean that their response is simply

a determined one."[22] For Frith, consumption is an ironic practice: one in which the dialectic of supply and demand/demand and supply problematizes the notion of cultural production and autonomy.

Frith and Hebdige owe much to Walter Benjamin, in that they share his view of popular culture as (and here I paraphrase Benjamin) a potential site for the masses to wrest tradition away from conformism, to exert their autonomy in the very act of "participation" in commodity culture.[23] Such a view of consumption as creation refutes Adorno's notion of "the philistinism of art as pleasure"[24] and foregrounds Frith and Hebdige's sense of youth's volatility, its tendency to *consume actively,* to *use* "in contexts of leisure and pleasure that are not easy to control"[25] the very commodities foisted upon them.

The Project at Hand

There is, in the final analysis, no one politics of youth and no one methodology that consistently applies. With that in mind and in hand, for the purposes of this study I have employed a flexible model drawn in large part from the various critical positions summarized here. It is not so much that I have sought common ground, but rather that I see youth as incoherent, ahistorical, riddled with continuities and contradictions that betray any attempt to render it singular or consistent or concrete. What follows then are a series of reflections and ruminations, an attempt to let the culture speak for itself in its very contradictions, in its very incoherence.

Much of this study is more suggestive than it is conclusive. This is by design. I am by no means claiming to advance *the* cultural history of youth. For now, we must be satisfied with *a* cultural history, one that examines a set of important texts as they intersect with a complex and contradictory set of social formations that loosely comprise the culture(s) of youth.

What follows is organized thematically: (Chapter One) alienation; (Chapter Two) deviance and delinquency; (Chapter Three) the politics of sexuality and gender; (Chapter Four) the politics of consumption; (Chapter Five) the apolitics of youth(ful) rebellion; and (Chapter Six) the regression into nostalgia. Each chapter disregards

7

chronology and embraces a cyclical model of history—one in which history is shown to repeat itself to different sets of material relations.

Throughout, I have resolutely resisted inserting a teleology of youth. For a culture that so resists definition, there are only versions, alternatives, alternative histories. History is never simple, never easy. This study clings to such an assumption to the last.

Chapter 1

The End of the World
(as we know it)

In "Kerosene," a song by the industrial-rock band Big Black, a group of teenagers feels so disconnected, so bored, they decide to set themselves on fire. It is for them, at least as the song's lyrics tell us, merely "something to do." Such, to appropriate a phrase coined by Edith Fass (by way of William Shakespeare), are "the children of our discontent."[1]

Alienation as a Social Problem

In his mid-sixties study, *The Uncommitted: Alienated Youth in American Society,* Kenneth Keniston writes: "A complex and heterogeneous culture like our own of course offers many different paths to acculturation; but insofar as ours is a culture, these paths share common, socially learned assumptions about what is important, meaningful and right. When this learning is incomplete, as with alienated subjects, we can speak of a failure of acculturation. On the most conscious level this failure of course involves the explicit rejection of most of the fundamental tenets of the 'American way of life.'"[2]

For Keniston, teen alienation is at once a psychological and social problem; it shows a disinclination to accept the inevitability of adulthood and a repudiation of the dominant values, roles, and institutions associated with adult society. Youth, in Keniston's view, often see themselves as caught between an idyllic and idealized past and an uncertain and uninviting future.

Though Keniston is tempted to view teen alienation as a form of psycho-social dysfunction, or at least as a transition phase in human development and social adjustment that one either grows out of or not, he goes on to argue that alienation must be seen as an instinctive rejection of the basic mores of the adult culture. Keniston's willingness to view alienation as an historical and political position is coincident with his sense of the failure of post-World War II society to offer teenagers all that much to live for. In Keniston's words, youth "desire[s] to find in adulthood the qualities of warmth, communion, acceptedness, dependence, and intimacy which existed in childhood; and one reason why this desire leads to alienation from adulthood is because adult life in America offers so few of these qualities."[3]

Such an idealization of youth and rejection of the inevitable future of adulthood leads to an overwhelming regret and sense of loss. Precisely because of this sense of loss, alienated youths consciously focus on the present. On the psychological front, Keniston points out that teen anomie engenders a distrust of commitment and an inability to achieve a stable identity, leading alienated youth to be characteristically ambivalent, apolitical, and uncommitted.[4] For Keniston, alienation is, when we are talking about teenagers, both the nature of *the* and the nature of *our* age.

Keniston's insistence on the social (rather than solely psychological) dimension of teen alienation foregrounds the prevalent contemporary reading (see Hebdige et al.) of teen anomie as a politically conscious refusal, a deliberate attempt on the part of youth to oppose the basic values of the official culture. And, to Keniston's credit, though he sees acculturation as a necessary and positive stage in human development, he concedes from the start of his study that, "our age inspires scant enthusiasm."[5] Three-hundred-and-eighty-eight pages later, he comes full circle. "Alienation," Keniston concludes, "is a response of individuals especially sensitized to reject American culture . . . and it is in part a response to social stresses, historical losses, and collective estrangements in our shared existence . . . given the existence of these stresses, losses and estrangements, it should not surprise us that our society inspires scant enthusiasm."[6]

Such scant enthusiasm—whether 1960s or 1980s style—underscores and is underscored by a profound nuclear anxiety. As Robin

Wood puts it in *Hollywood from Vietnam to Reagan,* "the characteristic and widespread sense of helplessness—that it's all out of our
hands, beyond all hope of effective intervention, perhaps already pre-
determined—for which there is unfortunately a certain degree of rational justification, is continually fostered both by the media and by
the cynicism of politicians." Wood's argument, then, leads to the
ultimate contemporary paradox: "'there's nothing you can do' (so)
'don't worry'."[7]

The post-Hiroshima paradox underscores the black and blank, anomic comedy *The Unbelievable Truth* (Hal Hartley, 1990). The movie
begins at the family breakfast table as Audrey, the film's wan, blasé
heroine, receives her acceptance letter from Harvard. Her father, a
loudmouth grease-jockey, gags at the University's five-figure tuition.
But he needn't worry. Audrey isn't matriculating because "the world
is going to end soon anyway." Instead, Audrey becomes an overnight
modeling sensation and falls in love with a mass murderer recently
released from prison. In the last scene in the film, Audrey and her
boyfriend sit down together and contemplate the future. But just as
the subject of Harvard crops up again, she hears something in the
distance—something that sounds like bombs heading their way.

Another recent film, *Miracle Mile* (Steve De Jarnett, 1988), ends
with the bombs actually bursting in air. Like *The Unbelievable Truth,*
the ending is a kind of bleak joke; the sky indeed is falling.

Nuclear anxiety similarly underscores the teen adventure film,
WarGames (John Badham, 1983). Far less comic than either *The
Unbelievable Truth* or *Miracle Mile, WarGames* offers a rather plau-
sible apocalyptic scenario: a precocious teen computer hacker penetrates a secret U.S. Defense Department computer and, thinking it's
just a game, sets World War III in motion. At the end of the film, the
teen hero comes face to face with the lunacy of Armageddon and
comes of age by repudiating the folly of his youth, the vanity of his
former apoliticism. He becomes a good citizen just as he becomes an
All-American adult hero: instinctively moral, charismatic, essentially
populist, and ultimately victorious.

The notion of youth saving the day, averting certain nuclear ca-
tastrophe, is also at the heart of the pre-teen picture, *Amazing Grace
and Chuck* (Mike Newell, 1987), a film that is at once politically

progressive and goofily naive. The film tells the story of a Little League pitcher who tours a missile silo with one of his father's friends. Stupefied, then radicalized, the boy refuses to pitch in the big game, or ever again for that matter, until the U.S. and U.S.S.R. disarm. Soon athletes from all over the world join his protest. At the end of the film, the boy gets his way, as the prospect of a world without sport is too much for those in power to bear.

Though *WarGames* and *Amazing Grace and Chuck* are essentially optimistic—in that the world does not end—both are, essentially, cautionary dramas. Both are predicated on the assumption of immanent disaster. And though it is youth who seize the day in both stories, both films presume a pervasive apolitics, apathy, and cynicism in American youth. Indeed, as Andrew Britton argues with regard to *WarGames,* films such as these "[calculate] brilliantly on the assumption that, while we are always being told, and may like to believe, that nuclear war is really just a game of 'Space Invaders' for grownups none of us is for a moment convinced of this."[8]

The Politics of Suicide

In the recent spate of teen films that focus on suicide—and there are a disturbing number of them—the apocalypse again emerges as a very real threat, a kind of degree zero for post-Hiroshima teen anomie. In these films, we who are not so young are told in no uncertain terms that it's just no fun being young anymore.

In *Pump Up the Volume* (Allan Moyle, 1990), Hard Harry, the local pirate radio station DJ becomes no less than a teen messiah simply because he unequivocally articulates just how lousy things can be when you're young. "We're all worried," he tells his listeners, "We're all in pain. High school is the bottom. Being a teenager sucks."

When a listener calls in talking about suicide, Harry is at first foolishly glib. But almost immediately the conversation turns ugly. The caller, indeed, means business:

Harry: (sarcastic) How are you going to it?
Caller: (serious) I'm going to blow my fucking head off.
Harry: (serious) Do you have a gun?

12

Caller: (sarcastic) No. I'm going to use my finger, genius. (And then he hangs up.)

After the caller's suicide, Harry deals with his own culpability, his sadness, and his own fears and death wish by venting his despair over the air. "Consider the life of a teenager," he says, "You have teachers and parents and TV and movies telling you what to do—The terrible secret is that being young is sometimes less fun than being dead." Describing teen alienation as a kind of no-man's land, he adds: "drugs are out, politics are out—we're on hold. We're the "why bother?" generation." For teenagers these days suicide is the bottom line; like the bombs Audrey hears throughout *The Unbelievable Truth*, it gives meaning to an otherwise absurd and meaningless life.

While the first two-thirds of *Pump Up the Volume* showcases Harry's anarchic, irreverent point of view, the final third (thanks to Nora, the campus heartthrob who seduces him) depicts his conversion to the very sixties' activism and political commitment espoused and formerly embodied by his parents. Harry's transformation from local curio to political rabble-rouser places the film within the familiar confines of the message teen melodrama. Rather simplistically, Harry's socially conscientious objection is pitted against idiotic, stereotypical, and palpably evil adult villains: an ambitious principal, her equally pernicious crony (the school guidance counselor), and a hotshot from the FCC (enlisted to enforce arcane restrictions governing the airwaves—and a symbol, in these post-Reagan times, of the idiocy of federal regulation).

But catching Harry is no easy chore. Armed with a portable transmitter, he eludes the FCC and the dumbfounded local police well into the night. By the time he's caught, the entire school is behind him. No longer so apathetic, his classmates similarly embrace the sixties' collective action they all had, theretofore, found passé and fairly humorous. (In case we miss the import of such a conversion, as the final credits roll, we hear the Sly and the Family Stone classic call to solidarity, "Stand," faithfully performed by the progressive rock band Liquid Jesus.)

In the final scene, Harry is carted off to jail. But he has a "great-looking" girl on his arm and the entire high school at his feet. Indeed,

he has achieved the kind of outlaw celebrity every teen dreams—or is said to dream—of. And while the film attends to its villains in various ignominious ways (the principal is fired by Harry's father in front of everyone, for example), there is no reason to tie up the narrative with regard to Harry. Whether or not he goes to jail is irrelevant because he has, in effect, already ridden off into the sunset of teen celebrity (however local and ephemeral). In the nineties, the makers of *Pump Up the Volume* seem to assert, celebrity may function as the only real antidote to the boredom and directionlessness of teen life.

The Apolitics of Murder

In a far different way, *River's Edge* (Tim Hunter, 1987) chronicles the "why bother?," "post-punk, pre-apocalypse" generation.[9] Here the consequence of teen anomie is shifted from suicide to murder, but the motivations seem quite the same. "Once you start fighting," notes John Sampson, the existential killer in the film, "you're always defending yourself. The whole world is going to blow up. What does it matter what I do?"

The murder of John's teen girlfriend precedes the film. It is shown only in (a clumsy) flashback and is of far less importance than how the murder "affects" the teenagers who subsequently protect John. When John's classmates are invited to "come on down" and view the corpse, their reaction is difficult to fathom. The girls seem apathetic. They say they want to call the police, but when they can't find a dime to make the call, they just forget about it. "I cried when that guy died in *Brian's Song*," one of them remarks, "you'd figure I'd at least be able to cry for someone I hung around with."

For John, the act of murder was, at the very least, not boring. "I felt so real," he says, "I felt so alive." But by the time Lane, the completely flipped out sort-of leader of the clique, offers to help John dispose of the body, John has lost interest and exits the scene. Though Lane is appalled at John's apathy, he takes care of the evidence himself. But his reasons for doing so indicate a bizarre set of values, culled from his favorite television shows (*Mission Impossible* and *Starsky and Hutch*) and the reductive history lessons on the network news. "It's people like you who are selling this country down the tubes,"

he says unironically, "no sense of pride—no sense of loyalty. Why do you think there are so many welfare cases? Why do you think Russia is gearing up to kick our asses?"

While Lane re-casts the drama of murder into a ritual of fidelity and togetherness, Matt, the film's reluctant hero, goes to the police. His betrayal, his heroism, is first set up visually when the entire group goes "down by the river" to view the body. As Lane occupies the foreground plotting a cover-up, Matt retreats further and further into the background, his head down, his eyes (like Harry's in *Pump Up the Volume*) never meeting the gaze of the camera.

Despite the inexplicable and inexcusable behavior of the teenagers in *River's Edge*, the film provides a rather pat explanation for why and how these teenagers could have been so cold and misguided. That the film places the blame on the parents is at once cliché and indicative of familiar sociological arguments regarding the roots of teen anomie.[10] Throughout the course of the film, we never see Lane's parents. Clarissa, the film's central female character and love-interest, doesn't seem to have a father and her mother is a joke in bad taste. Every time Clarissa either enters or exits the hallway that connects their rooms, we hear her mother repeat the same line: "Clarissa, is that you?" She never asks "Where are you going?" or "Where have you been?"[11] And she never leaves her room.

Matt's home situation is a single parent's nightmare. His younger brother is 12 years old, smokes pot, stays out all night, mugs Feck (the sixties counter-culture ex-biker—played by Dennis Hopper—who kills John), tosses his sister's favorite doll into the river, and nearly kills Matt (for "ratting out" John). Matt's mother is a nurse, apparently far too busy on the job to be of much use at home. Her live-in lover, Jim, abuses the kids and her as well. When things get tough, the mother shouts: "I give up this mother bullshit," and Matt, who has plenty of problems of his own, is charged with talking her down. When Lane drops by looking for Matt, he finds only Matt's little sister, home alone. "Where is everybody?," he asks. "Mommy's not home," she replies blankly, "Jim's at a bar. I don't have a daddy."

Cultural historian Robert K. Merton describes *anomie* as "a breakdown in the cultural structure" in which there is "an acute disjunction [between] cultural norms and goals [and the] capacities of members

of a group to act in accord with them."[12] At the core of the "breakdown in the cultural structure" in *River's Edge* is the dysfunctional suburban, nuclear family, presided over by ex-hippie workaholics and drug addicts. Given the disarray of the adult culture, the teenagers themselves cite a single group value of their own—fidelity—but it too is eventually abandoned and lampooned (via Lane) by the end of the film. Speaking to the importance of fidelity to the group—and murder is hardly unique as a factor in holding youth subcultures together, witness Charles Manson and the Family—Lane puts matters in the purest of teenspeak terms: "It's like a fuckin' movie when a good friend gets in potentially big trouble. Now we have to deal with it. We've got to test our loyalty against all odds. It's kind of exciting. I feel like Chuck Norris."

What makes *River's Edge* all the more disturbing is that it is based on a true story, one even more grizzly than the one told in the film. In 1982, in Milpitas, California, Jacques Broussard, then 16, killed his 14-year-old girlfriend Marcy Conrad and dumped her body in the woods outside town. At school the following day, Broussard openly boasted about the crime and led a dozen or so of his friends and acquaintances to view the body. One teenager dropped a rock on her face to see if she was really dead; another poked her with a stick (as Lane does in the film). While in *River's Edge* it takes Matt little time at all to have a crisis of conscience, in Milpitas, no one went to the police or to their parents.

Such stories of teen homicide are hardly unique. In Panhandle, Texas, for example, 19-year-old Kenneth Glenn Miller spent one steamy summer night (indicatively, Friday the 13th of July, 1990) murdering 17-year-old Freddie Garcia and attempting the murder of his ex-girlfriend's step-father and ex-high school principal. His room at home, police discovered, was wallpapered in teen horror picture posters. On the floor they found a clay corpse upon which Miller performed "special effects"—gruesome little performances with firecrackers and power tools that simulated scenes from his favorite films. The day before the murder he wrote in a friend's yearbook: "Your wisdom and advice have helped me out many times. Wish it could help with the problem I face now—wish I could tell you, but you'll find out sooner or later." The entry was signed "Damion," a mis-

spelling of the name of the child Antichrist in the horror film *The Omen* (Richard Donner, 1976).

Miller's peculiar problem distinguishing illusion from reality supports commonly held assumptions regarding how teenagers are affected by the often gruesome and violent "art" they so avidly consume. For those who believe that teen horror pictures and heavy metal music are a road to ruin, Miller's descent into violence and murder is a case in point. Indeed, no matter where we stand on the censorship issue—whether we see it as a matter of protecting or controlling the minds of the young—the role of teen-targeted media as an authority of sorts in many teenagers' lives seems hardly debatable any more.

In response to the ongoing lament regarding the sociological impact of teen sex and violence on screen and sensational(ist) stories about teen satanism, occultism, and the like, Wes Craven, the auteur of such classics (and Kenneth Glenn Miller favorites) as *A Nightmare on Elm Street* (1984), *The Hills Have Eyes* (1977), and *Last House on the Left* (1972), offers the following glib commentary:

> I believe we are at a fairly frightening, transitional stage in history. We tried the Ozzie and Harriet thing in the 50's, and that didn't work. We tried the hippie peace-and-love thing, and that didn't work either. We tried the yuppie thing, and the world got worse. So what's next? Today, there is no clear way for teenagers to go. All they have are politicians, TV preachers and cynical heavy metal musicians telling them things they sense are lies. No one is offering them the truth they crave so deeply. I make horror movies in which a character comes out of people's dreams and slashes away at anything that's bullshit. All I can tell you, I guess, is that I'm not surprised that Freddy Krueger is a teen hero.[14]

The role of the media in how teens view their own lives became an issue in Milpitas when a local theater planned to screen *River's Edge*. By then, Broussard had been caught, tried, and convicted. (He received a 25 years-to-life sentence, but was already eligible for parole.) The teenagers who ventured into the woods, but did nothing, were never indicted. Just how they live with the horror of what they saw and didn't do is anybody's guess. From its release, *River's Edge* was banned in Milpitas. Many residents claimed that they'd suffered

enough. Indeed, the effect the film might have had on the town five years after the fact is tough to predict. But its suppression again points to the issue of censorship and the problematics of what teenagers (seem to) want to see and what may or may not be "good for them."

Whoever or whatever is to blame for such extraordinarily wayward youths as Broussard and Miller is a difficult question. A provisional answer—one that disregards both the media and the family as the root cause of teen deviance—can be found in Elliot Leyton's *Hunting Humans: The Rise of the Modern Multiple Murderer.* Leyton argues that such seemingly unmotivated murders pose "a kind of sub-political and conservative protest."[15] Miller, in fact, fits Leyton's mass murderer profile to a "t": white, heterosexual, and male, unable to conform in spite of a desire to do so, summarily rejected by the very culture that produced him.

Employing Leyton's schema in a reading of *River's Edge,* Bryan Bruce concludes that John's crime poses "no threat to the established order."[16] "Attributing this 'conservative protest' to modern youth," writes Bruce, "tends to reduce teenage rebellion to the same apolitical terms that the heavy metal, death rock industry thrives on: senseless violence, nihilism, murder fantasies and an unmotivated and contrived rebel pose that has no material basis."[17] For Bruce, the very apolitics of it all—that John Sampson and Jacques Broussard were not motivated by or exploited by anything, really—is what is so disturbing about the film and the anomic youth it represents.

The apolitics of murder in *River's Edge* is affirmed in the film's cop-out ending as John is killed by Feck. Together they revisit the scene of John's crime and discuss the relative merits of murder. (Feck too has killed a girlfriend in the past.) When John quips, "I've got this philosophy: you do shit, it's done and then you die," he proves too existential for Feck's taste; he too is taken out of circulation, here via the all-American *deus ex machina* of a madman's bullet. "I don't like killing people," Feck crazily confesses to the camera, "but sometimes it's necessary." With a tear in his eye, he waves the camera away: "I lost a friend today, you know."

Such blank lunacy finds an apt counterpoint in the hyper-kinetic behavior of Lane, who cops a contrived rebel pose, wholly supported by the heady illusionism of the comic-book adventures on film and

television he so adores and the heavy metal music that blares on incessantly in his souped-up Volkswagen Bug. While both John and Feck are completely tuned out, Lane is totally tuned in. The role of the media (irrelevant for John and Feck, who kill; essential for Lane, who doesn't) seems at the very least very interesting.

Of primary import to any reading of *River's Edge* is an understanding of director Tim Hunter's critical distance, i.e. the tone of the film. For example, when the teenagers discover John's body in the river we hear a Hank Ballard blues number, "I'm gonna miss you," on the soundtrack. Earlier on, when they first go to see the dead girl, we hear Fats Domino's "There's a Thrill Up On the Hill." Too often the film is disconcertingly smug. It's hip because its view of today's youth is unflinchingly bleak.

Hunter seems similarly aloof in his work (as a director) on the television series *Twin Peaks*. There again his dispassionate realism and clearly defined critical distance depicts teenagers who seem to move through life (such as it is on *Twin Peaks*) with eerie disinterest, bound as they are in the show's trademark deadpan ennui.

Like *Twin Peaks*, Hunter's audience (for *River's Edge*) was at once targettable, limited and arguably not teen-age. In fact, while so many teen films were doing big business at the box office, *River's Edge* played primarily to the post-teen art-house market. As Gavin Smith argues in his review of the film, aptly titled: "Pretty Vacant in Pink," teenagers didn't "buy the film's implicit nihilism," preferring instead the far less real, romantic comedy world of *Pretty in Pink* (Howard Deutch, 1986). "The movie's whole point," Smith argues, "is that teendom is, for the vast majority, a wasteland of boredom, desperation and lack of purpose."[18] It renders such a state—such anomie—oddly glamorous for the liberal and hip and just a little too real for teenagers themselves.

Alienation and Conformity

To a great extent, *River's Edge* plays like an eighties remake of *Rebel Without a Cause*. Beneath the senseless violence and suicidal tendencies of the teenagers in both films resides a desperate need for

family (unfulfilled at home and only superficially satisfied by cliques and gangs at school). Both Matt and Jim Stark face a decision regarding the betrayal of their peers and both must make their decisions on their own. While Matt reluctantly takes on the responsibility of surrogate father (and fails pretty miserably), Jim becomes Plato's father-figure, but ends up watching his "son" die in his arms.

Both heroes seem overwhelmed by a pervasive alienation, but like Norman Mailer's "alienated hipster,"[19] their outsider status somehow signals their heroism. Despite the narratives they find themselves in, Keanu Reeves (Matt) and James Dean (Jim) transcend their circumstances by journeying inward, epitomized by the self-conscious "method" (school of acting).

Youth's aping (on the flip side of the screen), *en masse*, of the affected *angst* of such teen movie rebels signals how much more attractive tortured teen heroes (like Matt and Jim) are than their parents or teachers or the athletes, politicians, or any other adults who populate their world. Via the ever so self-conscious method, tough-teen anomie has emerged as a kind of glamour, akin to the strong and silent Western hero. Both, it is not stretching things to say, are male poses that signal something else again: a desperate need for rescue, in this case from a kind of hopeless and endless journey inward.

It is safe to say that after 1955, youth's resort to a kind of mannered anomie—on screen and on the streets—was patterned after James Dean's performance in *Rebel Without a Cause*. But Dean's anomic performance—his performance of anomic—which has become the most quintessentially American of youth cultural expressions, arose not from the ashes of the adult culture or from the spontaneity of youth subculture, but from the big screen, from the codes inherent to commercial Hollywood family melodrama.

Thus, we need to question what teen anomie as/like James Dean signified: separation or solidarity (all teens alienated together), collective resistance (empowerment, strength in numbers), or acquiescence to order and dominance (fragmentation, isolation, apathy)? Further complicating matters in *Rebel Without a Cause* is a nagging question that applies to the teen film in general. Given the parameters of cinematic narrative, can (for example) anomie really engender a

cultural refusal when it is, by virtue of its venue, undermined by a discourse (the Hollywood melodrama, in this instance) subsumed in the very power relations that oppress teenagers in the first place?

Dean's death within a year of the film's release, tragic and heroic as it was, lent further complexity and validation to youth's attraction to alienation and James Dean, as if they were, after his death for certain, one in the same thing. The mythos of living fast and dying young became quite popular but it carried with it the dubious Hollywood cautionary theme regarding the devouring nature of stardom and the safety of anonymity and conformity (of ultimately being unlike youth's shared ego ideal, James Dean).

Rebel Without a Cause opens with the teen hero, Jim Stark, drunk and disorderly, lying in the gutter. He is shot in distorted, wide angle, cinemascope close-up. The effect is a flattening of the depth of field, isolating the hero, the star, in the frame. In the subsequent scene in the police station, Jim rejoins the community of youth: Judy (with her red, red lipstick and cavalier manner) and Plato (an effeminate neurotic fresh off a senseless bit of brutality with some puppies). All three have spent the night alone. All three have gotten into trouble. And all three have been rounded up by the police for their parents.

Ray, the tough but kind police officer who is charged with returning these sad and lonely kids to their parents, comes to realize that his is no easy job. Judy tells him to call her father. He does, but her father's too busy, and her mother is sent in his place. Plato latches onto Jim (in fact Jim lends him his jacket, foreshadowing the climactic planetarium scene) and then is retrieved by his mother's black maid, who tells Ray that she's been "like a mother to the boy." Jim's family arrives from a party at "the club," already bickering amongst themselves. The room is abuzz with female energy: his mother mercilessly bosses his father and his grandmother bosses her. "How can a guy grow up in a circus like that?," Jim asks. "Beats me," Ray answers and offers his help anytime Jim needs someone to talk to.

Ray's offer is important for several reasons. In an obvious way, it shows within the context of the narrative that Ray sympathizes with Jim. His offer to listen fills in for what obviously does not happen at home. But, later on in the film, when Jim takes Ray up on his offer, Ray's not available (just like his parents). Likewise, in the opening

21

scene, Ray offers Plato a referral to a good psychiatrist—another professional authority to repair the damage done by a damaged family. But in the end, Ray instead oversees the murder of Plato by a trigger-happy fellow cop.

Like *River's Edge, Rebel Without a Cause* cites (and sites) teen anomie as primarily a family problem. And like *River's Edge*, it is hardly subtle about it. Jim wants his father to take control, to be a man. His father, instead, wants to be Jim's pal. One key scene in *Rebel Without a Cause* begins with Jim calling offscreen to his mother. Instead, his father, wearing an apron, emerges from offscreen and redundantly remarks: "You thought I was your mom?" Later, when Jim asks: "What can you do when you have to be a man?," it is obvious his father has no idea. When Jim is in deep trouble near the end of the film, he again seeks out his father's advice, but all he gets are blubbering remarks about making out a list. What Jim wants most is hardly the stuff of a rebel. He just wants his father to tell him what to do.

The film exploits the weak father figure to make its point regarding the failure of the suburban, nuclear family. Jim's father is an "organization man,"[20] a conformist at work (in some undefined and perhaps undefinable job) and at home. His failure to provide an adequate role model for his son, his failure to establish and maintain limits and to assert his authority, leads to his son's rather desperate anomie, which, narratologically at least, is the logical extension of his failure as a man.

Such a failure, and here we refer to manhood in the most conventional of terms, seems the direct result of his "other-directedness,"[21] his tacit acceptance of marriage and work, fidelity and conformity. Jim's father fits Barbara Ehrenreich's concept of the paradoxical "breadwinner and loser" fifties' male. Citing the work of feminist Charlotte Perkins Gilman, Ehrenreich argues that fifties' men were led "to love and care, to work, to serve, to be human." But following such a cultural directive essentially subverted their "male energy." Their sons, like Jim, were brought up principally by homemaker mothers, who, as a 1958 study revealed, made 60% of all the family's consumer purchases and managed the purse strings in 71% of all households. Such a family practice, Ehrenreich argues, led, inexor-

ably, to the wholesale rejection of this "new man" in the Beat, Playboy, and hippie philosophies, as well as in the no-place of the anomic teen.[22]

Loss of Self, Anxiety States, Anomie, Despair . . .

In "The Problem of Generations," child psychologist Bruno Bettleheim offers the following somewhat glib, but nonetheless perceptive allusion: "A youth expected to create a new but not yet delineated society finds himself a rebel without a cause."[23] It is pointless for youth to pursue goals, Bettleheim argues, when apathy is a kind of pragmatism, when parents' dreams of a future for their children beyond their own wildest dreams for themselves seem, to their teenagers at least, hardly interesting or possible. The breakdown of generational norms and values—destroyed by suburban leisure, the banality of the suburban nuclear family, and the cult of youth—leaves the young with nothing to fight for and nothing to fight against. "You cannot test your strength and vitality," Bettleheim writes, "the very things you are most dubious about as an adolescent, when all you can push against is a vacuum."[24]

Youth's "psycho-social" development is, as Bettleheim explains things, wholly dependent on the previous generation—in this case a generation that, in his view, had emerged from war embittered, and in many ways unable to cope with their own lives, let alone the lives of their teenage children. The net result of such a cultural breakdown is a mixed bag of signals regarding fidelity and diversity, community and individuality, family and selfhood. In a particularly glib update of Bettleheim, John Schowalter, 1990 president of the American Academy of Child and Adolescent Psychiatry notes: "When there's turmoil and social change, teenagers have a tendency to follow each other more. The leadership of adults is splintered and they're more on their own—sort of like *Lord of the Flies*."[25]

"It is the young," writes psychologist Erik Erikson, "who, by their responses and actions, tell the old whether life represented by the old and as presented to the young has meaning."[26] What one found in the failure of youth, Bettleheim and Erikson agree, was a kind of ritual dramatization of the failure of the generation before them.

Youth in the post-World War II period became a site for historical study, a site for political and psychological and sociological intervention, because adults seemed to project (onto their own kids and into motion pictures about other parents' kids) the very cultural discomfort that haunted them in the rapidly changing postwar era. In this way, the immediate postwar generation accepted failure as tacitly as they accepted the conformity that otherwise characterized their lives.

In the historical, sociological, and psychological literature contemporary to Bettleheim and Erikson—work by Erich Fromm, Erich Kahler, Fritz Pappenheim, Murray Levin, C. Wright Mills, David Riesman, Paul Goodman, William Whyte, Daniel Bell, William Kornhauser, and Kenneth Keniston[27]—one finds "alienation" identified as the principal malady (and principal point of entry into the study) of postwar society.

In the introduction to *Man Alone,* an anthology on contemporary alienation, Eric and Mary Josephson elaborate the following list of symptoms: loss of self, anxiety states, anomie, despair, depersonalization, rootlessness, apathy, atomization, powerlessness, isolation, pessimism, loss of beliefs and values, disequilibrium, strangeness, and dissociation."[28]

Such a focus on alienation as a core issue in cultural/historical research harkens back to Emile Durkheim, who argued that one could best study a society by focusing on those least served by it (e.g. those who felt or those who were purposefully alienated). Durkheim—and here we find the roots of the post-World War II psychology and sociology of adolescence—viewed alienation as emblematic of a dramatic breakdown in collective social values, a condition he described as "a normlessness," anomie.[29]

Durkheim's posit finds ample support in *Rebel Without a Cause,* a film that rather systematically depicts youth tragically alienated, unable to answer fundamental existential questions regarding the meaning of life and clearly indicative of a larger and collective cultural breakdown. In the opening police station scene, for example, Jim tells Ray: "I just want to hit someone. I don't know what to do anymore, except maybe die." Later on, Jim adds: "If I only had one day when I didn't have to be all confused—if I felt like I belonged someplace." When his parents argue over who's to blame for his problems,

24

he shouts "It doesn't matter" over and over. The following morning, when Jim and Judy meet outside her house, they exchange world views. "You live here?" he asks. "Who lives?" she responds.

The two planetarium scenes—the first gets Jim in trouble with Buzz, the second leads directly to Plato's death—offer a more diffuse, more global anomic message. In the first scene, the elderly curator gives a strange account of a forthcoming big bang. "Long after we're gone," he says, "the earth will not be missed. The problems of man seem trivial indeed. Man, existing alone, seems himself an episode of little consequence." To this chilling speech and accompanying special effects on the planetarium ceiling, Plato adds: "What does he know about man alone?" In the second scene, Plato asks Jim: "Do you think the apocalypse will come at night time?" and Jim responds, cryptically (but prophetically, at least for Plato): "No, at dawn."

The Crisis of Masculinity

The chickie run, the most shocking set-piece in *Rebel Without a Cause,* is but one of many games with death in the film. The teenagers—one and all—seem to regard death as a kind of tangible, empirical proof of life. (After all, who lives?) But while the chickie run is seen by the teenagers themselves as a ritual of machismo, heroism, and perhaps even rebellion, instead it confirms precisely what the teenagers claim to oppose—conformity, and in the meantime, boredom:

> Buzz: That's the edge. That's the end.
> Jim: Ya, it certainly is.
> Buzz: You know something . . . I like you.
> Jim: Why do we do this?
> Buzz: You have to do something, don't you?

Unluckily for everyone concerned, the run ends in Buzz's accidental death. Without Buzz, the Wheels (the school's ruling clique), are just mindless thugs. The in-fighting for authority within the group leads to paranoia (an apt allegory for McCarthy), violence, and more deaths. Judy, *sans* Buzz, latches onto Jim. In both paramours she finds

a *man* to take care of her, a role her father simply will not take on at home.

Though the film focuses a lot of attention on the issue of being a man, it does so uncritically. Jim's father means well, but he's weak; he allows himself to be bullied at home just as we gather he is bullied at work. Judy's father's insecurity is manifested in his inability to show her affection and in random and vain stabs at authority long after she has stopped listening. The key question of what to do when you have to be a man does not allow for a departure from the most traditional notions of manhood.

In *Rumble Fish* (Francis Coppola, 1983) and *Pretty in Pink,* two very different contemporary teen films, we find the weak father figure persisting into the 1980s. Abandoned by the women they married and still love, both men descend into the abjection of alcohol. For both fathers, alcohol abuse is both quintessentially male and tragic-heroic; despite their failure as parents, it is clear that the women who left them are to blame.

This "mother bashing" proliferates the teen film. Apropos Philip Wylie's controversial *Generation of Vipers,*[30] time and again we find bad mothers at the source of family discord and dysfunction. Indeed, they are the underlying reason behind the incapacitation of the once-heroic American male. In *Ordinary People* (Robert Redford, 1980), for example, the mother's inability to (show) love leads her son into the abyss of clinical depression. When, at the end of the film, the father finally stands up to her and she exits the scene, an all-male (and happy) family is formed.

In *Kramer vs. Kramer* (Robert Benton, 1979), a film about a pre-teen, the mother's impatience with the restrictions of parenthood prompt her to abandon her family as well. When she, in the end, prevails in the custody battle (read here as a weak society's empowerment of women) but then abandons her child (again, and for the better—for her and the child), she is a palpable villain. Her career is both the excuse and reason for the breakdown of the nuclear family and of the sanctity of matriarchy. In both *Ordinary People* and *Kramer vs. Kramer,* the male conquest of the home forces the bad mother into exile. In both films, wherever it is the mother goes is irrelevant. Such are the stakes for "liberated" women.[31]

The role of the father in contemporary cinema is far more complex and ambiguous. In the *Star Wars* trilogy for example, the future of a galaxy is held in the balance as we await the reconciliation of a single family's melodrama. The bond between father and son penetrates even the thickest armor. Darth Vader, once unmasked (in *Return of the Jedi,* Richard Marquand, 1983), speaks to misunderstood fathers everywhere. And in the end, his evil makes his son strong.[32]

A similar thematic emerges in *The Great Santini* (Lewis John Carlino, 1979), a film about an authoritarian and occasionally abusive and violent military man and his teenage son who is torn by the pangs of rebellion and an even more powerful urge to garner his father's reluctant approval. While the film chronicles the father's sociopathy, the lesson learned in the end (after the father's death in a plane crash), leads in quite another direction. The son discovers that his father's (superficial?) viciousness and unwavering discipline were his way of inarticulately dealing with his more vulnerable side: i.e. his fear of failure, femininity, and the otherwise inevitable breakdown of the family (all of which characterize the lives of "lesser" men). The rather rigid order he maintained when he was alive, then, was for the common good. Such extremism in the name of family need not be a vice.

By far the strangest father-teenage son scenario is played out in *A Night in the Life of Jimmy Reardon* (William Richert, 1988). Jimmy, the son, is an irresolute dreamer, a charmer with an eye on what he can't afford and what he is better off not having. The father is a tyrant, who, Jimmy discovers, has had an affair with his mother's best friend, Joyce (who, by the way, has just seduced him as well). The revelation of his father's indiscretion is at once shocking and reassuring to Jimmy. At the end of the film, as Jimmy and his father ride back home on the "L"—the symbol of everything Jimmy hates and fears (as it portends his future as a suburban commuter)—he and his father reconcile. The male bond is stronger than any facile morality either of them could choose in its place.

Rebel Without a Cause, like so many other teen films, reinscribes the family ideal despite its apparent failure for the teenagers depicted in the film. After Plato's death—the last in a series of climactic events in the film—Jim puts his arm around Judy and affirms that being an

outsider is not romantic at all. Intentionality aside, *Rebel Without a Cause* is both a critique of fifties' conformity and a film about "a rebel" conforming to some sort of family ideal, or ideal family. Only when Jim's father finally tells his mother to shut up and then puts his arm around *his* family can the film close off the narrative and the teenagers can finally stop killing themselves.

The search for an ideal family/family ideal is "staged" at the abandoned mansion near the end of the film. Plato arrives frantic after discovering a child-support check signed by his absentee father. Jim is on the lam from the factionalized Wheels, and Judy is with Jim because she can no longer be with Buzz. Plato play-acts the role of a realtor showing a home to two young marrieds played by Jim and Judy. When the conversation gets to the subject of children, Jim and Judy immediately respond that they don't want any. (Dean goes so far as to imitate Mr. Magoo, the familiar cartoon character whose voice is provided by Jim Backus, the actor who plays Jim's father.) We gather that the young couple feel the same way about kids they think their parents do: "so noisy," "we don't encourage them," etc.

Play-acting aside, Plato falls into a second role, that of Jim and Judy's son. It is an ironic twist of fate and narrative that Jim and Judy inadvertently abandon Plato just as his parents did when they split up. They tuck him into "bed" and then head upstairs to "explore." In their absence, Plato wakes to the sound of intruders, setting in motion a series of events that culminate in his death.

In the police car on the way to the mansion at the end of the film, Jim's mother remarks: "You never think about it happening to yours." That it does (to hers and to so many other mothers' sons) is precisely the message of the film.

Delinquency and the Search for Authority

The Wild One, a far different cautionary fable about wild youth released a year before *Rebel Without a Cause,* depicts parent-less youth cut off from (even dysfunctional) family life. The film stars Marlon Brando as a working-class, nihilist outsider; he is amazingly arrogant, oversexed, and as unlike Dean's sensitive son of suburbia as he could be. As Barbara Ehrenreich notes, Brando's Johnny epit-

omized a kind of fifties' male ego ideal, empowering the rigid, working-class, teenage male with the very masculinity a generation of fathers so obviously lacked.[33]

The Wild One opens with a disclaimer, a pre-title warning: "It's up to you to prevent this from happening elsewhere." In 1954, when the film was released, many in the audience were aware that *The Wild One* was based on a 1947 incident when motorcycle gangs took over and terrorized the town of Hollister, California. The film thus proved to be at once sensational and documentary, a combination that would come to characterize the 1950's teen movie.

At the beginning of the film, we see the motorcycle gang shot from overhead and from a distance. They appear quite like locusts on the horizon, poised to lay waste to this (or any such) lonely outpost if given the chance. Johnny, on the other hand, is introduced in a low angle close-up, and is never shown as part of the group. Though the camera signifies his difference, he insists he doesn't want to be leader. Indeed, when he's asked "What are you rebelling against?," he cryptically responds: "What have you got?" It's the key line in the film because audiences invariably find it hip. But narratologically it denotes his reluctance to take any real stand.

Despite its attention to a visceral, anti-social youth counter-culture, *The Wild One* is a very conservative film. Its many allusions to the movie Western—its attendance to such themes as civilization versus the wilderness, progress versus ethical responsibility, the breakdown in law and order and the necessity for a strong leader (e.g. a sheriff) to seize the day—indicate its ideological similarity to such (other conservative) fifties' films as *High Noon* (Fred Zinnemann, 1952) and *Shane* (George Stevens, 1953).

The failure of institutional authority in *The Wild One*, as in the Wild West, relates a dysfunctional, weak society. For example, the town's policeman attempts to befriend the gang. But it backfires. They see only his fear and he becomes like most of the terrified adults in the film, their patsy. The local cafe owner—the arbiter of capitalist entrepreneurship and progress—decides to exploit the situation; but he too underrates the teen menace. When he sees the gang ride into town, he gleefully remarks: "Better put some beer on ice." But he soon rues the day, as the gang takes over and trashes his establishment.

A far more successful authority emerges when the no-nonsense sheriff from out of town arrives and arrests Johnny. Refusing to sentimentalize or try to understand the anomic teen, he characterizes the strong and silent, anti-heroic Johnny as no more than a brutal thug, as essentially a criminal (even though Johnny hasn't committed a crime and the sheriff does not have a legal right to hold Johnny against his will).

"I don't get your act and I don't think you do either," the sheriff says. Then, shifting gears, he adds: "I don't know if there's good in you, but I'm willing to take a chance." So long as Johnny understands the rules, understands the rationale for adult male authority, he is "free" to go.

As a teenager (in fact or at heart), you can't watch *The Wild One* and not side with Johnny, not reject the sheriff as yet another symptom of the problem with the older generation. In this its infant stage, the teen film emerges (already) at cross-purposes: providing a reassuring or alarming, or reassuring and alarming message to adults while at the same time providing an irresistible and charismatic, anti-social rebel hero for its young (at heart) audience. Though the narrative attends to the rescue and restoration of the adult society (somewhat smarter now for having lived through the siege), Hollywood's priority on stars, and Brando's ability as a star to seize the day (to dominate the screen), sets *The Wild One* up to be as paradoxical and ambiguous as the culture it attempts to re-present.

The same can be said for *Rebel Without a Cause*. It too is a very conservative film. But like Brando, Dean transcends the narrative, his image redefining a story that is very much at his (and the teen audience's) expense.

From Ruin to Romance

At the heart of the difference between *Rebel Without a Cause* and *The Wild One*—two films that in retrospect have come to "represent" much the same image of youth—is the way the two narratives regard the heterosexuality of their respective heroes. In *The Wild One*, for example, the love affair between Johnny and the waitress is straight out of the movie Western. She is, in essence, a potential obstruction

to his freedom; she signifies the very adult society he flees, the very responsibility and domestication Jim Stark in *Rebel Without a Cause* so desires.

Though she represents what Johnny thinks he does not want, the waitress is at the same time the only one who really understands him. "It's crazy," she says, "you're afraid of me and I'm not afraid of you." His smoldering machismo, she knows, is just a pose (lampooned to great effect in the independent gay classic *Scorpio Rising* [Kenneth Anger, 1962–63]). To an extent because he is surrounded by willing and able "biker-chicks," when Johnny meets the waitress he is instinctively afraid of what showing his real feelings could do to him.

"I want to touch you," the waitress says, "I want to try." But he can't let her. When the sheriff lets him go, Johnny ambles out without saying a word. "At least say thank you," the sheriff says to him. But she responds instead: "He doesn't know how." But he does. In the film's sentimental denouement, he returns to the cafe, alone, sits across from her for an inordinate amount of time, says nothing, then cracks a smile. He is, we discover (and this would become a cliché in later teen films), a tough guy with a tough past and a (well-concealed) soft heart (i.e. the ultimate working-class hero). Weird as this may seem, Johnny, moreso than Jim Stark, is the hope of the future—a man's man in a society seemingly overrun by women managing men's childhoods, later their homes, their finances, and their sex lives as well.

In *Rebel Without a Cause*, the stakes of romance are quite different. Judy's first line in the police station is "He must hate me—He called me a dirty tramp," to which Ray adds, "Do you think your father meant it?" With the appropriate teen *angst*, she responds "Yes, no, I don't know." Later in the conversation, Ray repeats the father's accusation: "You weren't looking for something [walking the streets], were you?" She was, but not what they think—not what they fantasize about and are troubled by.

Though in a private moment we see Judy frown at her image in a mirror, she is, publically at least, the prize for which the boys in the film compete. At the chickie run, we see her ecstatic smile as she drops the flag. When the headlights hit her and the wind rushes by and her dress swirls up, it is clear that she doesn't mind it one bit.

This not so subtle public display of sexuality is an exception to the otherwise rather somber ambience of the rest of the film. (Even cinematically, the chickie run is the only scene that has any real life.) Indeed, when Jim and Judy go upstairs at the mansion, they may well be planning to have sex, but they go about it only after play-acting as a married couple.

The Nostalgia for Authority

Brando and Dean, who in our collective memory have come to represent youth in the 1950s, were, at the very least, very serious. But as they have been re-presented in such nostalgic works as *American Graffiti* (George Lucas, 1973) and the TV series *Happy Days*, they appear hopelessly romantic, emblems of a lost machismo that seems by now fairly humorous and anachronistic.

The drag-racing legend John Milner in *American Graffiti* is, beneath the thinnest veneer of cool machismo, tired and morose; his James Dean-like pose is systematically undercut throughout the film as he is victimized by a wise-cracking fourteen-year-old girl. Fonzie, all but an institution in the seventies, was introduced on *Happy Days* as a Brando-like biker, threatening Richie, the show's bland hero, into helping him cheat on an exam. But as the show persisted, and this is typical of the false class reconciliation of situation comedy on television, Fonzie eventually became part of the absurd and banal Cunningham family, accepting its values and diluting his masculinity in the process.

Quite a different nostalgia is achieved in Terrence Malick's *Badlands* (1974), a film that loosely retells the real-life story of Charles Starkweather, who, with his girlfriend Carol Fugate, went on a killing spree (that began with her father) in the mid-fifties. While the times depicted in *Badlands* seem simpler, they also seem stupider and crueler. The incredible vapidity of the film's heroine (and narrator) underscores the banality of nostalgia.

When Kit, the stand-in for Starkweather, is introduced, it is through her eyes (clouded as they are by the teen magazines she reads incessantly). "He was handsomer than anybody I ever met," she says in characteristic deadpan, "he looked just like James Dean." In his

own peculiar way, Kit too is starstruck; his dreams of gaining notoriety (to replace his boredom and anomie) are realized, however ironically, in a police car as the Texas Rangers escort him for extradition:

> Ranger: Kit, . . . you like people?
> Kit: They're OK.
> Ranger: Then why did you do it?
> Kit: I don't know. I always wanted to be a criminal, I guess. . . . just not this big a one. Takes all kinds, though.
> Ranger: (to his partner) You know who that son of a bitch [Kit] looks like? I'll kiss your ass if he don't look like James Dean.

The camera returns to Kit who, like Brando in the final scene of *The Wild One,* for the first time in the film, cracks a smile. Clearly, the Ranger has made his day.

More contemporary allusions to *The Wild One* and *Rebel Without a Cause*—films like *River's Edge, The Boys Next Door* (Penelope Spheeris, 1986), *Suburbia* (Penelope Spheeris, 1984), *Over the Edge* (Jonathan Kaplan, 1979), *Less Than Zero* (Marek Kanievska, 1987), *Heathers* (with its lead male character J.D., aka Jason Dean), and *Permanent Record* (Marisa Silver, 1988)—present a far darker nostalgia. They depict, as Gavin Smith puts it, "absurdist nihilism [as] the Eighties' prevailing style—an inverted glamour adopted by kids as they indulge in the peculiarly narcissistic masochism of adolescent self-martyrdom."[34]

At the far end of teen anomie one finds the rationality and rationalization of suicide, an alternative to coming of age that renders the prevailing romantic view of anomic youth absurd. In a number of contemporary teen films—*Permanent Record* and the far more commercial *Dead Poets Society* (Peter Weir, 1989) to name just two—we see good kids (with "everything to live for") retreat into themselves, face the absence of meaning out there in their lives, and kill themselves. But what does such self-sacrifice, such a refusal to come of age, say about the adult culture? Charles Ricks offers the following provisional answer: "There is something improbable about there being a whole phase of life that embodies nothing but disadvantage. The more open way to come at it is to ask: along with the disabilities

and mawkishness of adolescence, what truths about life is the adolescent better stationed to see than either the child or the man?"[35]

J.D. Salinger's 1951 *The Catcher in the Rye*, long a rite-of-passage novel for American youth, begs the same question. At the end of the book, Holden Caulfield may well discover that he has been right all along. Everyone is (more or less) a phoney. But his descent into alienation does him no good at all. That he sees things accurately is precisely the problem. For Holden, the logical extension of teen anomie lay in the despair and futility of madness.

In a classic bit of understatement, Kenneth Keniston quips: "From a psychological point of view, alienation and privatism can hardly be considered ideal responses to social change."[36] Yet, he laments, estrangement is increasingly *chosen* as youth's reaction to the world around them.

Why American teenagers, from the 1950s to the present, have so often opted to withdraw into alienation—at least as the teen film presents things—has at its source several cultural determinants, which, taken together, form a Spring cleaning list for 1990s conservative America: (1) the failure of adult society to provide adequate role models; (2) the absence (due to significant cultural, political, and economic change) of discernable and tradition-bound rites of passage into adulthood; (3) the adult generation's refusal to grow up (the descent into suburban leisure, the persistence of rock and roll); (4) the celebration of youth as the *sine qua non* of contemporary happiness (the pervasive nostalgia for one's own youth that seems to elide just how difficult it is being young); and (5) the irresistibility of particular filmic role models (e.g. Dean and Brando) who have rendered anomie hip.

The notion of anomie as hip brings us full circle, not only back to Keniston's reference to "a society engendering scant enthusiasm," but back to the bleak lyrics of contemporary progressive rock and roll. By way of conclusion, consider the following paean to today's aimless and hopeless youth, written and performed by REM, chorus as follows: "It's the end of the world as we know it/And I feel fine."

Chapter 2

The Path of the Damned

During the celebrated Tate-LaBianca murder trial, Charles Manson offered the following testimony: "I never went to school, so I never growed up to read or write so good. So I have stayed in jail and I have stayed stupid and I have stayed a child while I watched the rest of the world grow up and then I look at the things you do and don't understand. My father is the jailhouse, my father is your system . . . I have done my best to get along in your world and now you want to kill me and I look at you and then I say to myself: You want to kill me? Ha! I'm already dead. Have been all my life. I've spent 23 years in tombs that you built."[1]

For those who study deviant youth—and in the study of youth culture such a focus dominates the field—Manson offers a compelling case study. Born on November 12, 1934 in Cincinnati, Ohio, the illegitimate son of 16-year-old Kathleen Maddox, Manson grew up believing his birthday was November 11; his mother vaguely remembering that his birth occurred sometime around Veterans Day. During Manson's youth, Maddox lived with a succession of men. One, a much older man named William Manson, was around long enough to give her son his last name.

Several stories persist regarding Manson's biological father. The first tells of a Colonel Scott (first name unknown) who, in an "agreed judgment" in a bastardy suit, consented to pay Maddox $25 plus $5 per month support (an agreement he, by the way, never lived up to). Some years later, in Ashland, Kentucky—less than three months before the Tate and LaBianca murders—a motorcycle riding guru from California calling himself "the Preacher" (answering to Manson's general description and accompanied by a coterie of female followers)

the seventies, a decade populated with "permanent cripples [and] failed seekers" all clinging to "a desperate assumption" that some sort of messianic authority lay at the end of all the ceaseless and selfish soul-searching.[6]

In addition to his discussion of Leary, Thompson foregrounds Manson by citing the Beatles' embrace of the Maharishi ("like Dylan going to the Vatican to kiss the Pope's ring"). As Thompson concludes: "First gurus, then Jesus, then Manson and his primitive instinct lead." Such "a blind faith in some wiser and higher authority" was where the sixties was headed all along, Thompson argues, a point made all too clear as the seventies rolled around and the "doomstruck era of Nixon" began.[7]

Though far more of a conventional historian, William O'Neill shares Thompson's seventies' cynicism. In *Coming Apart,* his "informal history of the sixties," O'Neill argues that the Family was the logical result of a kind of alternative authoritarianism, "the repressed hostility, authoritarianism, perversity and mindless paranoia that underlay the hippie ethic." The hippies and flower children were "natural victims and natural victimizers," O'Neill glibly concludes, and "the Manson Family were both at once."[8]

Indeed, as the sixties wore down, "the rhetoric of the young got progressively meaner and more hostile." While the Family, the Black Panthers, the Students for a Democratic Society (the S.D.S.) and the Weathermen openly and at times violently rejected the official culture, all three groups succumbed to the very authoritarianism they otherwise rejected in the culture at large.[9]

As to his followers, Mansons' power over them remains a disturbing reminder of the still ongoing lure of youth cults. Dr. Joel Hochman, the psychiatrist who examined Susan Atkins upon her arrest, analyzed her as follows: ". . . at this time we might suggest the possibility that she may be suffering from a condition of *folie à famille,* a kind of shared madness within a group situation."[10] After observing Atkins on trial, Los Angeles *Times* reporter David Smith remarked: "Watching her behavior—bold and actressy in court, cute and mincing when making eye-play with someone, a little haunted when no one pays attention—I get the feeling that one day she might start screaming and simply never stop."[11]

If Manson had an extraordinary perceptiveness or cultural saavy, it was displayed in his ability to coopt (and render somewhat coherent) the vast array of seemingly paradoxical fads and political crosscurrents crowding the air in the American sixties. In addition to the systematic subjugation, con-game manipulations, persecution/ paranoia-based fear, and rigid patriarchal authority of prison life, Manson was (to varying degrees) influenced by (and thus adopted tenets from): Scientology; the Process (a radical political, proto-religious organization); Catholicism (picked up at Boys Town); Protestant fundamentalism (culled from his aunt and uncle); Hopi Indian mysticism; the pop psychology of Eric Berne; (his favorite novel) Robert Heinlein's *Stranger in a Strange Land* (which tells the story of an amoral superman, complete with harem, mind-reading powers, and designs on world domination); and the then very popular music of the Beatles.

Manson's charisma, or at least his ability to marshall the manipulative skills he learned in prison, made him more than a match for his aimless and all too amiable flock. In rituals of resistance of an astounding sort—acts of mutilation and murder that reside at the furthest end of delinquency and deviance among the young—the Family repudiated the faltering official culture of the American sixties. But on a more micro-cosmic level, it was Manson's psychological need to control and his followers' search for authority—their apparent need for dependence—that underscores this infamous chapter in American youth cultural history.

The Sociology of Delinquency

In *From Teenage to Young Manhood,* Daniel and Judith Baskin Offer discuss the psycho-social development of adolescents via four "fundamental perspectives of normality." These perspectives (which, in their words, "represent the total behavioral and social science approach to normality") include: (1) "normality as [good] health" (a psychological approach in which behavior is considered normal in all cases in which psychopathology does not exist); (2) "normality as utopia" (a sociological approach in which normal behavior indicates optimal functionality, perhaps even happiness); (3) "normality as

average" (a behavioral approach based on a mathematical model in which any and all extremes of behavior "reside outside the normal range"); and (4) "normality as a transactional system" (a "bio-psycho-social" approach in which normal behavior is seen as the end product of "interacting systems" taking into account the complexity of stimuli in the lives of normal teenagers).[12] But despite such a complex machinery of the study of "normality," for the Offers (and for the vast majority of those who seriously study youth culture), normal teenagers are of little interest.

The focus on deviant teenagers similarly characterizes the "new sociology" of youth. Dick Hebdige, Stuart Hall, John Clarke, and Phil Cohen,[13] for example, all argue that the sociopathy of deviance and delinquency is inherently politically progressive. Citing the failure, or the brutality, of various institutions charged with the socialization of youth (the family, the church, the school, the mass media), these sociologists posit that deviance indicates "a breakdown in consensus." Deviance and delinquency, then, is (seen as) a kind of ritual(ized) refusal, a form of inarticulate protest emblematic of larger problems the adult society is unable to reconcile.

But what is missing in this new, progressive sociology of youth is how deviance, in and of itself, puts in a call for a stricter and surer authority, how deviance itself is pre-figured in the "floating equilibrium" of hegemonic, post-World War II culture.[14]

Surely the most dramatic expression of teen deviance is delinquency—the very extreme behavior the Offers, for example, hope to cure and the very dramatic "refusal" that in the new sociology signifies youth's most profound state of alienation and impatience. Correspondingly, delinquency has become another site for intervention, an excuse for the implementation of institutional authority in the socialization of wayward youth.

In his influential study, *Causes of Delinquency,* Travis Hirschi argues that "delinquency is not caused by beliefs that require delinquency, but rather is made possible by the absence of (effective) beliefs that forbid delinquency."[15] Such a liberal politique aptly characterizes the majority of wild youth melodramas.

Over the Edge (Jonathan Kaplan, 1979), for example, a B-teen-movie about out-of-control teenagers ritually vandalizing public and private property in a hideous planned community predictably places

the blame on adults from the very outset. "This story is based on true incidents," the opening titles tell us, "in a planned community of condominiums and townhouses where city planners ignored the fact that a quarter of the population was 15 years old and younger." In such a simplistic sociology, these teens' vandalism is, as Hebdige suggests (via Norman Mailer), an imprinting of their mark on their parents' space.[16] From such a point of view, and given the sterile, uniform architecture throughout the community, vandalism seems more a matter of taste, an aesthetic rather than criminal act.

Though *Over the Edge* engages us on the side of the rebellious teenagers, it denotes and de-problematizes the inevitability of their socialization, their acquiescence, their suppression and punishment. The film climaxes with the unruly teenagers laying siege to their high school with the local community council trapped inside. The scene has a kind of party atmosphere, not unlike the ending of the far less earnest *Rock 'N' Roll High School* (Alan Arkush, 1979). The adults are so ridiculous, so hateful, so stupid, we hardly care what happens to them. Rather, we share a kind of euphoria in the anti-society of the young, which here seems an altogether appropriate response to the banality and corruption of "culture" as represented to them by their parents.

But once the fire is put out and the adults are released, the film turns unironically moralistic. As order is restored, the film's unlikely hero, the teen introvert Carl, is nabbed by the police as he exits aimlessly from the school grounds. In the subsequent scene—a de-nouement which neatly frames the narrative—we see Carl's friends perched up on a bridge (the very bridge where, at the start of the film, two teenagers fire a BB-gun at a police car), waving to Carl as he is carted off to a juvenile home. On the soundtrack we hear the plaintive: "Oooh child/Things are gonna get easier." It is, in the end, the provision of authority, signified by the paddy wagon, that re-writes the rest of the film. As the narrative plays itself out, Carl not only gets what he deserves, he gets what he desires.

Re-Contextualizing Delinquency

Every day, 135,000 teenagers in the United States bring a gun to school. Every thirty-six minutes, a youth is killed or seriously injured by a bullet. "We like to think in terms of good kids and bad kids,"

quips John B. Waller, Jr., the Director of the Center for the Prevention of Interpersonal Violence at Wayne State University in Detroit, "but the only difference between a victim and a perpetrator is who gets off the first shot."[17] In keeping with such a glib sociology—especially Waller's implicit point that any and every youth is a potential perpetrator and/or victim—in recent years the mass media has reductively focused on the spectacular emergence of the teen gang as the principal manifestation of wild youth gone deadly out of control.

In *Colors* (Dennis Hopper, 1988), for example, we see the gang supplanting the unstable families, inadequate schools, and no-future job opportunities of the East LA ghetto with an almost tribal family togetherness. The gangs are popular because they provide disenfranchised youth with a formalized sense of belongingness and fidelity. But while *Colors* grimly attends to the problem of teen gangs, it does so in the peculiar parlance of the Hollywood urban adventure film. As a result, the gang characters, good and evil, are charismatic, romantic, even mythic. The white buddy cops are cut in the *Dirty Harry* mold. Though they are plenty tough, they are also sadistic and racist. By reverently depicting the gang's code of conduct, its cultural unity and seductive outlaw lifestyle, the film ends up endorsing their "culture," since it seems far more progressive than the culture represented by the white police.

Public outrage at *Colors'* apparent romanticization of the gangs was understandable, predictable, and exploitable. The Guardian Angels, for example, picketed selected screenings of the film. Geraldo Rivera and Phil Donahue spectacularized the film's celebration of the gangs via the peculiar realism (as promotion) of the television talk show. But despite its mythic romance and exploitation picture release strategy, the film aptly displayed the problem itself: in the absence of alternatives, the gangs are attractive.

The Warriors (Walter Hill, 1979), released a decade earlier, provoked a similar public outcry. Paramount's ad-slicks for the film pictured well-armed and well-costumed gang youths above the following chilling caption: "These are the armies of the night. They are 100,000 strong. They outnumber the cops 5 to 1. They could run New York City." But the promotional campaign was misleading. *The Warriors* was not really about a teen gang takeover. Rather, it too is a pat

Hollywood adventure picture depicting good gang-bangers and bad gang-bangers. The plot does concern a struggle for authority over the city. But the struggle is clearly between the youths themselves, not between the police and the gangs. Unlike *Colors,* the code the gangs cling to is revealed to be empty, easily betrayed, and hardly useful. While the posters promise something truly ominous, the film instead chronicles a series of carefully choreographed rumbles and last-minute rescues. In the end, the notion of youth pooling their resources is rendered absurd.

The Politics of (Teen) Violence

In his introduction to the 1988 edition of *A Clockwork Orange,* Anthony Burgess quips that "senseless violence is a prerogative of youth, which has much energy but little talent for the constructive."[18] Such a sour view rather characterizes the novel, with one important proviso: that, eventually, Alex (the delinquent hero) grows up and his penchant for violence is revealed to be "juvenile and boring." "It is with a kind of shame," Burgess concludes, "that [Alex] looks back on his devastating past." As he begins to grow up, he realizes "he wants a different future."[19]

In 1962, when *A Clockwork Orange* was first published in the United States, it was comprised of twenty chapters, one fewer than virtually every other international edition. Stanley Kubrick's 1971 film adaptation of the novel is based on the twenty chapter version, and in doing so disregards Burgess's "weary and traditional"[20] moral lesson regarding free will and random violence. Kubrick's film revels in Alex's "ultraviolence," using slow and fast motion and a synthesized classical score to aestheticize the violence (as choreography, as cinematography, as pure imagery). Burgess's novel is far more of a cautionary allegory. "There is, in fact, not much point in writing a novel," Burgess argues, "unless you can show the possibility for moral transformation."[21]

Both the film and the novel chronicle Alex's fortunes with regard to the vagaries of authority. Things begin with him in charge; as he puts it: "There has to be a leader. Discipline there has to be, right?" Eventually, his authority is challenged by his gang: "No more picking

on Dim. It's part of the new way." Subsequently, Alex re-seizes authority by beating his "droogs" into submission. But the following night, he is betrayed, left helpless for the brutal police.[22]

After his arrest, Alex's (subcultural) authority is unsuccessfully challenged by the prison warden, the guards, and the chaplain. Indeed, Alex remains unchanged until he volunteers for Ludovico's Technique and is "cured" of his violent impulses. But he is also cured of his ability to exert free will. The transformed Alex is not only dehumanized, he becomes, instead of the perfect Christian as the government promises, the perfect victim. And he is paid back for past transgressions first by old men, then old friends, and finally by an old nemesis, his namesake F. *Alex*ander, the writer who plans to use him for political ends.

It isn't until the end of Chapter Twenty in the novel and the end of the film that Alex is restored to his former self and we are left to feel a perverse euphoria at his ironic victory. Structurally, Alex's authority as a first person narrator and central figure in the narrative is never undermined. His victory at the end of Chapter Twenty—his return to who he is (a brutal thug)—finally matches content with form, narrative with narration.

The twenty-first chapter moves things in quite another direction. On the streets again with a new gang, Alex confesses "I felt very bored and a bit hopeless."[23] He meets an ex-droog in a coffee house which prompts "a sudden like picture" of himself sitting in an armchair before a roaring fire. "Youth must go," he concludes, "But youth is only being in a way like it might be an animal. No, it's not just like being an animal so much as being like one of those malenky toys you viddy being sold in the streets, like little chelovecks made out of tin with a spring inside and then a winding handle on the outside and you wind it up grr grr grr and off it itties, like walking, o my brothers. But it itties in a straight line and bangs straight into things bang bang and it cannot help what it is doing. Being young is like being one of these malenky machines."[24]

Burgess's return to the image of "a clockwork orange," something alive yet also mechanical, here relates not so much to Alex, the unfortunate victim of the state and its bio-chemical brainwashing, but rather to Alex the quintessential (wild) youth. "All it was was that I

was young,"[25] Alex remarks near the end, and with such an unsatisfying sentiment, he daydreams about a wife and kids and a little job
someplace. In exerting his free will he opts for conformity. It was
what all the rest of the novel had been leading up to.

A Tribute to Our Communities and Our Faith in Youth

Though Alex's socialization—which, pointedly fails—is accom-
plished through the most violent means of state control (the penal
system), by and large it is the school, with its ample motive and
opportunity, that is brought to bear in the socialization of (even such
wild) youth. Successful socialization, though, is a double-edged sword.
And the shifting institutional emphasis from "education" to behavioral modification is, of course, problematical.

Describing the product—the graduating senior—of such an institutional education, Jerry Farber sardonically notes: "They've learned
one thing, and perhaps only one thing during those twelve years.
They've forgotten their algebra. They've grown to fear and resent
literature. They write like they've been lobotomized. But, Jesus, they
can follow orders."[26]

A graphic case-in-point of Farber's observation can be found in
Frederick Wiseman's 1967 documentary, *High School*. Shot in suburban Pennsylvania at a white, middle-class high school, Wiseman
went into the film hoping to expose what he foresaw as a growing
resistance in the "next generation," feeling, by then, a first wave of
discontent at the absurdity of Vietnam. Instead, Wiseman found a
disconcerting apathy, students sleepwalking in an atmosphere that
seemed not only antiseptic but anaesthetic.

In *High School,* as in his subsequent films *Hospital* (1970) and
Welfare (1975) for example, Wiseman found himself analyzing an
institution not as it serves its constituency but rather as it institutes
its ideology. At Northeast High School, the day begins with the "daily
word" on the loudspeaker, a reductive aphorism about citizenship and
hard work being its own reward. Throughout, we find teachers obsessed with hall passes and arcane, baffling regulations: the principal
discussing girls' skirt lengths, an English teacher reciting "Casey at

the Bat'' while her students doze off to sleep, another English teacher playing a tape of Paul Simon's "Dangling Conversation" (a song about a breakdown in communication) while her students stare glassy-eyed at her reel-to-reel tape recorder (that is, indicatively, playing the song back at the wrong speed) and a Spanish teacher repeating "un philosopho existentialista" over and over again with her class, effacing the phrase's content while emphasizing its pronunciation (and hence its utter meaninglessness). The students learn, and I use that term guardedly, by rote and repetition. In effect, the school strips virtually everything of its context and fragments the students' experience to the point of incoherence.

The overt, authoritative, and authoritarian role of the school comes across in the disciplinary principal's office as, early on in the film, we see a student ably protest his innocence. Accused of disrupting his class, it is obvious he is blameless and it is equally obvious that the administrator believes him. But the boy is assigned detention anyway. "We want to see," the administrator says, "if you're a man and can take orders."

Later, in a sex-education forum for girls in the school auditorium, a gynecologist lectures that "promiscuity is the worst thing in our society" and concludes her presentation with the following pernicious aphorism: "You have learned by now, by being human, that you can't have what you want when you want it." Should such subtlety escape us, Wiseman concludes the documentary with a final, chilling vignette. We share with the camera a seat in the audience at a faculty meeting. A home economics teacher reads a letter from a former student, "a young man who was unexceptional in every way." He is, she tells us, about to embark on a suicide mission in Vietnam. In the letter's most telling passage, he concludes. "I'm just a body doing a job." Then, as the camera zooms in slowly, the teacher unironically states the school's bottom line. "When you get a letter like this," she says, "it means we are successful here at Northeast High School."[27]

In 1967, the College Board Achievement Test in English offered the following essay topic to some 130,000 High School seniors: "The trouble with open mindedness is that your brains could fall out." The responses were, for those unprepared for the worst, disconcerting indeed. "If you once open your mind," writes one student, "all sorts

of bad ideas can drop in and you might end up a narcotics attic [sic]."[28] A survey of the essays denotes a generation obsessed with success and conformity (like today), preoccupied with fears of drugs, atheism, communism, and being caught with their standards down.[29] "What they all want," writes Fredelle B. Maynard, "is security, in particular, the security that comes of guidelines firmly drawn . . . The greatest single complaint in these papers—one finds it again and again—is that parents and teachers have abrogated their natural authority for a wishy washy 'what do you think?'"[30]

The prototype youth problem/school problem film is *The Blackboard Jungle* (Richard Brooks, 1955), a rather uncompromising melodrama focusing on the growing menace of juvenile delinquency in inner city high schools. The film proved at once prescient—if things were not so bad in 1955, they got that way soon thereafter—and controversial. Indeed, its rather too graphic depiction of the growing j.d. menace prompted several localities across the United States to ban the film. In Memphis, for example, one censor called it "the vilest picture I've seen in 26 years."[31] And though *The Blackboard Jungle* was selected as the official U.S. entry at the Venice Film Festival, it was pulled by the State Department.

To quell the uproar, most prints of the film carried the following message-movie disclaimer: "We in the United States are fortunate to have a school system that is a tribute to our communities and our faith in American youth. Today we are concerned with juvenile delinquency—its causes—its effects. We are especially concerned when this delinquency boils over into our schools. The scenes and incidents here are fictional. However, we believe that public awareness is a first step toward a remedy for any problem. It is in this spirit and with this faith that *The Blackboard Jungle* was produced."

Though it does attend to the racial and economic factors that impact on the problem of juvenile delinquency, *The Blackboard Jungle* is primarily concerned with how teen deviance not only "boils over into our schools" (where, after all, it's just teen against teen), but how the criminality of discontented youth effects and invades the adult world. When, for example, a math teacher brings in his much treasured swing records to elaborate a mathematical principle, the students mock him and smash his collection. When Mr. Dadier (the teacher-

hero) gives a lecture on racism, the students deliberately misunder-
stand him (perhaps because they know better) and report him to the
principal. The irrelevance or naivete of such lessons are juxtaposed
to the absolute authority of the streets: of teen gangs, broken families,
and the prevailing hopelessness of the inner city.

Early on in the film, Dadier is mugged in an alley by some of his
students. But when the police arrive to question him, he refuses to
"rat them out." The local policeman, who, like Ray in *Rebel Without
a Cause,* is both hard-boiled and benevolent, tries in vain to break the
code of silence with the following words of wisdom: "I've handled
lots of problem kids in my day," he says, "kids from both sides of
the tracks—they were five and six years old in the last war—father
in the army—mother in the defense plant—no home life—no church
life—no place to go." But Dadier is unmoved and blankly replies "I
gotta go teach." Forlorn, the cop concludes his sermon on a rueful
note: "Maybe kids are like the rest of the world today: mixed up,
suspicious, scared."

The discontent at the core of delinquency is elaborated by the film's
principal antagonist, Artie West. "A year from now," he says, "the
army comes along, and they say Artie West you get on a uniform and
you get your lousy head blowed right off. Or maybe I get a year in
jail and when I come out, the army, they don't want Artie West to
be a soldier no more. Maybe what I get is out." For West, delinquency
is not the site of ruin or romance. In the absence of viable alternatives
to gang rule, West decides to make the most of his leadership potential. To a certain extent Dadier understands the situation, but he feels
it is his role to do something about it.

Throughout the film, Dadier, ever the heroic teacher, tries to reach
West. But to the film's credit, it is the teacher who comes of age on
this score and learns that some kids are unreachable. After school
one day, Dadier follows West out into the street. There he watches
as West's gang pulls off a heist. "You're in my classroom now," West
quips, "and what I could teach you . . . You don't get to flunk out
here."

At the end of the film, West pulls a knife on Dadier. He is easily
subdued as the majority of the class turns on him. When the knife
falls into the hands of one of his cronies, Belazi, he too is thwarted,

this time by Santini, "the idiot boy," who rams him in the stomach with an American flag (a metaphor lost on no one in the audience then or now).

Why Can't Johnny Read?

"In principle," writes Paul Goodman, "every teenager is a delinquent . . . and our preferred means of keeping them on ice is to keep them usefully in school."[32] The problem Goodman rather glibly elaborates is not so much "why can't Johnny read?" but what can we do to keep him off the streets? and for how long?

This notion of youth incarcerated, or at least detained at school (in the best interests of society), is echoed by Farber, who argues that schools "solve an existential problem."[33] For youth, time is a most problematic and plentiful commodity. School, then, offers a kind of structure later filled by work and family.

Cultural historian Kaspar Naegele furthers this argument, positing that public education provides the state with "a means for establishing a wider social order."[34] Deviant youth, then, both signals the failure of the school to socialize adequately and fuels the notion that discipline and order are what teenagers need; indeed, it's also what they want.

In the recent teen film, *Lean on Me* (1989), we find *The Blackboard Jungle* recast in contemporary urban New Jersey. Directed by John Avildsen of *Rocky* and *The Karate Kid* fame, *Lean on Me* is a strange combination of right-wing Libertarianism and Capra-esque populism—a glorification of a lone, eccentric hero whose success is the only ideology of concern in an otherwise complex world.

Like *The Blackboard Jungle, Lean on Me* begins with opening titles affirming its position *vis à vis* the dread and fascination, the news of youth gone out of control: "Once considered among the finest high schools in America, East Side High School of Paterson New Jersey declined over the years until an official report called it a terrible cauldron of violence. The battle of one man, Joe Clark, to save East Side High School and restore its former pride is the subject of our story."

Lean on Me shares several plot elements with *The Blackboard Jungle.* For example, "Crazy Joe" Clark, the school principal, beats up a boy who attacks him with a knife and in doing so wins the respect of his students. In another scene, he confronts some bad kids in the bathroom (which is where Dadier first confronts his nemesis, the black underachiever, Miller) who turn out not only not to be so bad but (like Miller et al.) also to be good singers.

But in a far less sophisticated way, *Lean on Me* offers the solution to the problematic relationship between education and delinquency. In *Lean on Me,* the solution is Clark, the HNIC (the self-proclaimed "Head Nigger in Charge"). At his first faculty meeting, for example, Clark insists on his role as an all-knowing authority, a moral force in an otherwise immoral wilderness. "No one talks at my meetings," he shouts at his colleagues, "You can take out your pencils and write. I want the name of every hoodlum, drug dealer, and miscreant who's done nothing but take this place apart on my desk by noon today." Once given the list of names, he kicks them all (all three hundred of them) out of school.

Clark ends the meeting as he began it, shouting: "This is not a damned democracy. My word is law. There is only one boss in this place and that's me." Clark is the self-proclaimed Dirty Harry of the American education system, further evidence of the perverse power of the popular (but how is it populist?) cinema of conservative reassurance that prevails in America today.[35]

While the solution to the problem at the East Side High, we are told, is simple enough—after all, as Clark maintains, "Discipline is not the enemy of enthusiasm"—Clark's ideology is hopelessly contradictory. While he tells the faculty, "if you treat them like animals, they'll behave like animals," he chains the students inside the school (under the pretense of locking local dope pushers out) and hires an armed security force (to protect them from themselves). He remarks that "self-respect permeates every aspect of (one's) life," but then humiliates a fat, black boy about his clothing in front of a lunchroom full of students. He makes all kinds of populist statements, like "the only way to get anything done is to get everyone involved." But he doesn't mean it. He knows best, and that's the bottom line.

With ample box office success, it is clear that Avildsen knows how Americans, *en masse,* like to see themselves. In these narratives of

little guys overcoming all odds, there is an implicit fascism. The cure, time and again, is the "right" man for the job.

Clark's peculiar brand of authority smacks of sound bytes and television evangelism. When, for example, he accepts the job as principal, he claims to see lightning and hear thunder. (There is a little of both Jesse Jackson and Al Sharpton in Clark's appeal.) "This is a war," he tells us, "a war to save our children."

The children are looking for a savior. And Clark is exactly what they want—someone to get down into the trenches, a man who won't waste time trying to understand them. In the wild rally that ends the film, we see, in no uncertain terms, the triumph of absolute authority, the kind the kids all crave: Crazy Joe, who, despite interference from the petty bureaucrats of the state (Clark is a Reaganite hero through and through), roams the halls from 6 AM to 6 PM, watching, watching, watching, locking them in or out, protecting them from themselves and the possibility that they may grow up to be drug "attics."

Like *Lean on Me*, *Stand and Deliver* (Ramon Menendez, 1988) displays how tough love can help tough kids. Also based on a true story, *Stand and Deliver*—and do note how the title implies the power relations in the film—is about a classroom of East Los Angeles teens who are mercilessly pushed by a self-less teacher in an A.P. course in Calculus. Like Clark, this teacher sacrifices his health and private life in the basically thankless task of educating inner-city youth.

But when the students in *Stand and Deliver* perform well on the national A.P. test, the establishment tries to put them down. And though the teacher, the moral center of the film, stands by his kids, ETS, which administers the test, maintains that the whole class cheated and forces them to take the exam over again.

Like *Lean on Me*, *Stand and Deliver* is patently populist. When the students retake the test, they again do well. But on another level, the students' and teacher's triumph is muted by the educational establishment's incipient racism. Such, in the end, are the obstacles to a true multicultural America, and the film hardly pulls its punches on that account.

In Paul Mones's little seen *The Beat* (1988), rival gangs in an inner-city school find a temporary reprieve from their ugly lives in the magic of poetry, a spark first set by a dedicated, if overmatched teacher,

and then by a strange, messianic new student. *The Beat* is arrogant enough to be optimistic without being reductive, ascribing a liberatory power to art in the ongoing drama of deviant youth. As in *Lean on Me,* the adults in *The Beat* have abandoned all faith in their offspring. Thus, like the end of virtually every juvenile delinquent/high school film, it is up to the teenagers to affirm a faith in themselves. Such is the prevailing populism of post-World War II America; teens need to do for themselves what their parents, teachers, and government have given up trying to do for them.

The Politics of Education

"In the pre-war period," argues C. Wright Mills, "the prime task of education was political"—e.g. citizen's education: making young people aware of their future rights and responsibilities in a democracy. But in the postwar period, characterized by Mills as "the mass society," "the function of education shifted from the political to the economic";[36] and a priority was placed on training people for a growing international market economy.

Ironically, such a shift empowered the schools all the more. Today, the question, "why can't Johnny read?" not only regards the nagging problem of illiteracy, but the problematics of a world economy in which the United States has failed to maintain control. Youth's descent into delinquency—into the abjection of deviance, refusal, and anomie—then exceeds, as a problem for public policy, the parameters of domestic concern over criminality and interpersonal violence. Far more important is a kind of internationalist agenda in which a retooled education system, with youths who are adequately socialized to function in the global economy, will most certainly play a significant role.

There is, though, another tack we can take on this. Given three basic alternatives at school—functionality, resistance, and failure—we need to ascertain how each "alternative" prefigures an entrance into, marginality to, or alienation from health, wealth, and the pursuit of happiness in the future.

It is fair to say that the global economy depends on a certain percentage of failures, an underclass left behind, just as it depends on a

certain elite class that benefits from its largess. It is daunting, but nonetheless unsurprising that the selection process begins with children and adolescents. If indeed education is the key to success in the global economy, the institutionalization of a culturally divided education here serves a truly significant socializing function. Such are the politics of American education in the last years of the twentieth century.

(This notion that society depends on a certain percentage of failures also impacts on the issue of juvenile delinquency. As Michel Foucault argues in *Discipline and Punish*,[37] society maintains control by identifying a certain percentage of the population as dysfunctional or anti-social. Punishment, then, is at once a social imperative and part of a culturally distinct symbolic order. In such a scenario, juvenile delinquency does not undermine society; on the contrary, a certain number of delinquents are necessary to the ongoing maintenance of order.)

With the notion of a culturally divided education system in mind, consider the astonishing popularity of two recent polemical books on contemporary education: Allan Bloom's *The Closing of the American Mind: How Higher Education Has Failed Democracy and Impoverished the Souls of Today's Students* and E.D. Hirsch, Jr.'s *Cultural Literacy: What Every American Needs to Know.* Bloom's focus on the authority (if not the authoritarianism) of a restrictive University-educated elite corresponds to a domestic shift to a service-oriented economy in which there is a coincident need for experts (peopled by the afore-mentioned elite) and, though he does not say so in so many words, a discernable (permanent) underclass. For Bloom, these days the problem is that there are too many chiefs and not enough Indians.[38]

Hirsch, like Bloom, blames our education woes on an overly diversified system, but with an important political twist. "Literacy," writes Hirsch, "is not just a formal skill, it's also a political decision."[39] Shared, canonical knowledge, Hirsch argues, is "necessary to a literate democracy." Hirsch's brand of "citizen's education" includes: (1) the promotion of acculturation (read here socialization, ethnic erosion, and assimilation); (2) the placement of a value on selected American mores (but which ones?); (3) the teaching of a specific set of standardized historical facts (e.g. "DNA, the first amendment, Grant and Lee"); and (4) the institutionalization of a

"canonical cultural knowledge" (in which a centralized board of regents institutes education rather uniformly across the nation).[40]

In effect, Hirsch glibly accepts that socialization is the primary function of our schools. He sees no problem in using the system to get people back on the right track. The popularity of both Hirsch's and Bloom's peculiar fascisms testifies to widespread frustration over the failure of our schools and our young.

Both Hirsch and Bloom bewail youth's inability to fathom or care about history or literature. But they ignore what it is that youth does know, what it is they do care about. Both books deal with youth as essentially deviant and malleable and in doing so offer agendas for our culture that are alternatingly racist, sexist, and inhumane.

Socialization and Refusal

"Youth are inevitably regarded as a problem,"[41] Geoff Mungham and Geoff Pearson muse in "Troubled Youth, Troubling World," their telling study of deviant youth in the U.K. But the problem with such an approach, as Mungham and Pearson aptly point out, is that it forces "us" to look at youth as if it were a problem to be solved, as something (e.g. Bloom and Hirsch) that can or needs to be fixed.

Such an historical approach—such a cultural directive—leads back to the problematic issue of socialization, that the failure of the young identifies a failure of the generation in power to coerce youth into their way of thinking (e.g. the failure of institutionalized, public education to enforce, or at least re-inforce, the authority of the ruling class). With that in mind, consider the following counter-argument posed by Marty Jezer in his insightful postwar history, The Dark Ages. "A rising rate of juvenile delinquency, along with a growing cult of violence, was the first indication that the socialization of young people was not going well," writes Jezer, "or, put another way, it was going too well, and the young were learning the underlying values of postwar society while ignoring the glossy suburban image that supposedly represented the real thing."[42]

In his sociological study of America's young and aimless in the 1960s, Growing Up Absurd, Paul Goodman shares Jezer's sense of

irony with regard to the paradoxical effect of socialization. "It is not that troublesome youth are undersocialized," Goodman concludes, "perhaps they are socialized perfectly well. Perhaps the social message has been communicated clearly to the young . . . and it is unacceptable."[43]

Chapter 3

The Way of the Beautiful

In the opening classroom scene of *Where the Boys Are* (Henry Levin, 1960), Merrit, the film's almost-too-smart-for-her-own-good heroine, challenges her college professor in a class on courtship and marriage. While the elderly, out-of-step teacher drones on about "random dating" and "premature emotional involvement," Merrit reduces the whole course to a single pressing question: "Should a girl, under any circumstances, play house before marriage?"

The answer Merrit provides is an unequivocal yes. And when she cites the Kinsey report as her primary source, she is kicked out of class and sent to the dean's office. "We are not here to discuss Dr. Kinsey," the professor bristles, "We are here to discuss interpersonal relationships."

Kinsey's effect on post-World War II America is difficult to underrate. A biologist by training, Kinsey's effort to disconnect the study of human sexuality from the vagaries of cultural taboo and abstract morality was coincident with an earnest scientific interest and a careful scientific method. But once *Sexual Behavior in the Human Male* and *Sexual Behavior in the Human Female*[1] were re-presented in the daily newspapers and popular magazines of the day, Kinsey's "report," as it came to be known, was widely viewed as primarily an ideological tract.

A decade later, William H. Masters and Virginia E. Johnson published *Human Sexual Response*. Unlike Kinsey, whose data was culled from almost 20,000 personal interviews, Masters and Johnson compiled their data from films (they supervised) of men and women masturbating and having intercourse. Coincident with their (then) alarming clinical methodology, Masters and Johnson rather purpose-

57

fully characterized their findings as the hallmark of an impending "sexual revolution," one which promised to alter traditional gender roles and sexual practice. In an indicative bit of purple prose, Masters and Johnson affirmed "(an) incredible swing from yesterday's Victorian repression to today's orgasmic preoccupation"[2]—a cultural shift heralding both the sexual emancipation of women and the onset of a society obsessed with performance and personal gratification.

Much like the focus on alienation and delinquency in the cultural history of youth, the study of sexuality evinces an ongoing lament regarding an out of control, changing society. (That nostalgia would be the refuge of the 1970s and 1980s has its roots here.) Vance Packard, in his best-seller *The Sexual Wilderness,* argues that the changes set in motion by Kinsey primarily regarded issues of gender, not just sexuality, and that these changes portended no less than an end to patriarchy, an end to society as we know it. "You cannot overhaul the status of one sex," writes Packard, "without altering the status of the other in the process. Consider the matter of relative power. If a woman gains in power, the man quite obviously must give up some, and make the best of it, or fight back."[3]

Citing the chaotic state of "interpersonal relationships," Packard characterizes "the sexual wilderness" as "the whole range of areas where males and females find themselves in confrontation."[4] The primary drama in this battle of the sexes, Packard argues, is that women have been acting and men have been reacting. Such an imbalance, then, engages a "demasculinization" of culture, an erosion of male authority, and an accompanying breakdown in cultural norms attending to the sexual activities of the young. Packard blames: (1) a decline in parental control; (2) a marked decrease in general community scrutiny of young people; (3) the wavering role of religious doctrine; (4) the increased availability of effective means of birth control; and (5) a growing unwillingness among collegiate authorities to act as substitute parents.[5]

For Packard, the erosion of culturally instituted structures of power and authority evinced a naive progress model of history. In the fast lane to posterity, America had lost control and its youth had gotten lost with them.

By 1967, 40% of America's college age youth enrolled in college and 40% of them were women. As youth's role in the larger culture

changed, Bruno Bettleheim noted an apparent "extension of adolescence" and a coincident absence of tradition-bound rites of passage
into adulthood.[6] Anthropologist Margaret Mead shared Bettleheim's
view. "We actually place our young people in an intolerable situation," she argued, "giving them the setting for behavior for which
we punish them whenever it occurs."[7]

In the late sixties and early seventies, the sexual revolution was
widely viewed as intrinsic to and responsible for youth's descent into
drugs, Eastern mysticism (cults), feminism, homosexuality, hippie
bohemianism, and political radicalism. Sex became the *cause célèbre*
in the celebrated generation gap.

From Romance to Rape

The extension of dependence, and thus youth, is a problem the girls
all face in *Where the Boys Are*. Before they embark for Florida and
Spring break, Melanie lies to her father, telling him she will be in
Chicago with her friend Angie. Merrit tells the dean that she needs
to get away because she can't talk to her parents, "at least not about
things that really matter." Not a single parent appears in the film,
despite the fact that they are footing the bill for the vacation.

Merrit's speech regarding pre-marital sex in the opening classroom
scene sets two oppositional dramas in motion: naive Melanie's descent
into promiscuity and subsequent victimization and Tuggle and Merrit's ongoing battle to remain chaste. That they are all playing adolescent games in adult bodies is clear enough to everyone concerned.

Merrit's struggle to remain chaste clearly runs counter to her intellectual acceptance of the theoretical foundations of the sexual revolution. She is, the film posits, like a lot of coeds in the U.S., a victim
of her own rational, developing intellect and of society's affirmation
(via college) of equal opportunity. For example, when Ryder, her
paramour, tells her she's a good kisser, she being frosh queen and
all, Merrit takes it as an insult. "No girl likes to be considered promiscuous," she says. But he counters with a line straight out of sociology
class: "Sex is no longer a matter of social norms." That saying yes
(on her part) has something to do with what happens in the classroom
is hard to miss.

When Ryder comes on strong, Merrit puts him off with a treatise on "the three types of boys," all "interested in the same thing": (1) the sweepers (who sweep you of your feet); (2) the strokers (who use soft music and soft light); and (3) the subtles (who use the intellectual approach). But it is clear that Merrit is just putting up a front. Though she is and plans to remain a good girl, she can't explain why.

When Ryder finally accepts what he will and won't get from her—such are the stakes of their relationship after all—he offers a rather conservative and adolescent course for their relationship. After inviting her to his graduation dance, he provides the straight line for the film's unsubtle message: "You're a strong girl, Merrit," he tells her. "No girl is," she replies, "when it comes to love."

Though we take the goofy, gangly Tuggle far less seriously than Merrit—Merrit after all is studying Russian vocabulary when Ryder picks her up on the beach—her relationship with TV, the film's flamboyant clown, takes a very similar course. After their very first night out together, Tuggle talks about "getting fit for a belt," that "he keeps knocking at the door and it's only a matter of time while I keep the door locked."

Seated on adjoining chaise lounges by the motel pool at the end of their first date, Tuggle already feels compelled to make the big confession, that, though she doesn't want to disillusion him, she is, and plans to remain, a good girl. At first, TV perseveres. It is his role in the culture to do so. But when it becomes apparent that Tuggle will not give in, he "strays" with a much older exotic dancer named Lola. But in the very act of ditching Tuggle, TV has a crisis of conscience. After Tuggle runs off crying, TV abandons Lola, and then, though we get sidetracked by the film's most disturbing sexual drama, we gather TV spends the rest of the night tracking her down to apologize.

Early on in the film, in a scene that rather obviously marks the intellectual differences between Tuggle and Merrit, Tuggle looks to the future. While she sees a bright future for Merrit, she accepts that she is built for just one thing, her destiny as "a walking, talking baby factory." That she, even more so than Merrit, decides to put off such a future—that she clings to her adolescence (here defined by sexual inexperience, because such are the rules of the game for girls in youth culture)—seems a very smart idea indeed.

Melanie's fall from grace is both inevitable (in that we see it coming) and shocking (in that the light comic tone of the film hardly prepares us for just how far she falls). After just one day of independence from parental, community, and collegiate authority, Melanie defers to Merrit's speech in class on interpersonal relationships. After one date, she is smoking cigarettes. After another, she is hopelessly drunk and says to Merrit, "You were right!" But Merrit recants and relegates Kinsey to the classroom, where, we gather, he belongs. "I was talking about people in general," she says, "not kids who go out and get drunk together." But Melanie insists, "I know what I'm doing." Of course, we know—we've seen it before—she doesn't.

Melanie, ostensibly "the pretty one" in the group, is immediately targeted by two boys staying at the same motel. While she is swimming, we see the boys flip a coin to see who gets to take her out first. Eventually, they take to trading her back and forth. And then one of them rapes her.

The rape scene is shockingly realistic, a timeless and timely depiction of date rape. It takes place in a seedy motel out on the strip. Melanie waits for Franklin, who stands her up. His friend, and her ex-boyfriend, Gil, shows up in his place. The camera stays on her as she backs into the room, repeating, softly, over and over again: "No, no, no . . . ." We then cut to the sorry aftermath. Gil is gone. Melanie's dress is torn, her manner, almost comatose. She calls Merrit (of course) who is out with Ryder. Instead, she gets Tuggle, who is back at the room crying because of TV and Lola. Tuggle exits the room and eventually finds Merrit and Ryder on the beach just as Merrit is about to "give in." The three of them get into Ryder's car and eventually "rescue" Melanie who they find wandering somnambulistically headlong into traffic.

In the hospital scene that follows, the film turns even darker. The police seem hardly interested as they take down the boy's name and address. Melanie's doctor leaves her room smoking a cigarette and smugly remarks that "she'll get by." Merrit, understandably, feels a lot of guilt at this point and also realizes how close she came that night to falling prey to her own foolish advice.

Though the girls exit college with boys on their mind—thus expecting not to spend a lot of time together unless they are unlucky—

Melanie's rape establishes a bond amongst the girls the boys can't hope to penetrate. Though he essentially means well, when Ryder repeats the doctor's lame reassurance that Melanie will be all right, he becomes the target for Merrit's rage: "I suppose you want me to thank you [for saving Melanie], but I'm not feeling very grateful right now." "Are you going to blame me," Ryder whines, "for what somebody else did?" "I blame all of you who think of a girl as something cheap and common," she replies, "put here for your personal kicks." Though they reconcile at the end of the film, it is clear that there is nothing productive he or anyone else can say. For Melanie—and for all those girls out there like her—it's just too late. Such are the rigid set of compensating values in *Where the Boys Are*. Though the film hardly blames Melanie for what happens, it also unambiguously regards her as beyond redemption.

Indeed, when Merrit visits Melanie in her hospital room, their conversation affirms the irreversibility of the tragedy and the necessity to search for rescue from the most traditional of authority figures, Melanie's father:

> Melanie: I goofed it up. I should have died. Why didn't I die?
> Merrit: Everything's gonna be all right. As soon as you get back to school . . .
> Melanie: (interrupts) No, not school I want to go back (pause) to my father. I want to go back to my father and mother. They'll tell me what to do, won't they?
> Merrit: Sure they will.
> Melanie: I feel so old.
> Merrit: It's not the end of the world. You'll meet somebody—some nice boy, back home.
> Melanie: Some nice boy? (sarcastically) And I'll tell him all about my wonderful Spring vacation. He'd like to hear that.

The scene ends with a close-up of Merrit, reassuring her friend that "it'll be all right," though it is clear that she and we know it won't be. Merrit's advice and Melanie's reliance on her authority has led to disaster. Left to their own devices, this "bunch of live it up kids," as Melanie describes them, make a lot of bad decisions. That Melanie needs her parents to tell her what to do is a lesson she learns too late, and that is the real message at the end of the movie.

Girls and Subcultures

When the girls in *Where the Boys Are* go South for Spring break, leaving the security of their all-girls' school behind them, they attempt entry into the already ongoing male youth culture; after all, that's "where the boys are." But the rite of passage into such a youth culture is restricted to a kind of sexual negotiation the girls just can't win. Melanie, who submits, ends up losing her youth. (She complains that she "feels old" in the hospital.) Merrit and Tuggle, who resist temptation, remain outside and are left to wait for proms and dances, phone calls and a proposal down the line. For them, youth culture remains where the boys are and where, because of what they have to do to stay, they are not.

In "Girls and Subcultures," Angela McRobbie and Jenny Garber argue that as young girls search for a strategy for "negotiating their concrete, collective experience," they manifest—they for the first time formalize—their marginalization in contemporary culture.[8] "It's not so much that girls do too much too young," writes McRobbie in "Settling Accounts with Subcultures: A Feminist Critique," "rather they have the opportunity of doing too little too late." Should girls want to participate in the progressing (if not progressive) culture of youth, McRobbie posits, they need to establish their own subculture(s) which like the boys', prioritizes the bond of friendship with their own gender over their relatedness to, their interest in, their marginalization from subcultures otherwise dominated by boys.[9]

For ten-to-fifteen-year-old girls, there is refuge in the almost totally pre-packaged "teeny-bopper" culture. As McRobbie and Garber describe it, teeny-bopper culture is: (1) easily accommodated (it requires only a room and a record player); (2) flexible (it is not exclusionary at all, unlike clique-ruled high school); and (3) without risk (of being stood up, of not being asked to dance). The "quasi-sexual ritual" of dreaming about teen heartthrobs, those sad and pretty boys who sing maudlin songs about puppy love gone bad, establishes a solidarity with the very young girls they otherwise, or will soon, compete with for boys. In the girls' obsession with particular stars, McRobbie and Garber find "a meaningful reaction against the selective and totalitarian structure"[10] that dominates their lives at school.

In the not so small act of choosing their own objects of fantasy, girls locate their subculture inside the bedroom, an ironic space in that its surrender will someday signal their adulthood. From early adolescence, then, girl subculture is pushed underground, or at least inside, rendering it (quite unlike boys' subculture) invisible, inaccessible, and clandestine. Girls learn early on that sexuality is far more important to their subculture than it is for boys and they learn, like the girls in *Where the Boys Are,* to keep what happens there secret.

Dick Hebdige's view of subculture as a formalized and progressive performance of cultural resistance is not incompatible with the argument regarding girls' bedroom culture.[11] If we view the retreat into the bedroom as a ritualized response, a negotiation of an untenable socio-sexual dynamic in which girls are forced to act contrary to desire, in which they represent, or are, the object of so much of the ritual content of the far more active group-oriented male youth culture, we can see girls' subculture as, in McRobbie and Garber's terms, "a resistance to what can at least in part be viewed as their sexual subordination."[12]

As young girls move out of the bedroom, one finds sexuality the central issue once again. While boys bond in protracted rites of male solidarity, girls assemble cliques whose sole purpose is to exclude other girls (a point hyperbolized in films like *Heathers, Some Kind of Wonderful* [Howard Deutsch, 1987], *Pretty in Pink,* and *Carrie* [Brian DePalma, 1976]). Given no group identity (outside the bedroom) and no public forum (except publicity regarding private sexual activity), girls may well not manifest any clear markers of public identity and as such end up "apparent" only in their subordinate roles in male subcultures or as the object of study, the site of permissiveness and deviance, in alarmist forays into the cultural ramifications of sexual practice and politics among the young.

Negotiating the Sexual Wilderness

When Vance Packard surveyed 2100 college students in 1966, attempting to horrify his readership with evidence regarding the wanton sexual behavior loosed by Kinsey and Masters and Johnson, he focused his study on young women. But, much to his disappointment, he found

"no indication that copulation had become rampant among college women." In fact, he found a "solid majority" were still virgins. What Packard also discovered was that intimacy had become more egalitarian (e.g. an increase in mutual genital petting and a "spectacular decline" in male students' "use" of prostitutes).[13] The study revealed a marked increase in intimacy among "social equals," an unforeseen result of the very shift in relative power between the genders he so feared.

In *Teenage Sexuality,* published nearly a decade later, Aaron Haas similarly found youth to be far more conservative and responsible than the tremors of moral panic over a sexual revolution had led him to expect. Haas's study found that only 42% of the boys and 41% of the girls had had sex while still in high school[14]—data that rather resembled Packard's. In a 1990 sampling, the average age for first intimacy for those with experience dropped from eighteen to seventeen—from the first year of college to the last year of high school. This strikes me as hardly a significant change from Packard's study in 1966.[15]

In response to questions regarding what they want most out of life, sixties and eighties college students overwhelmingly cite careers, success, and money. As to what they want most from a mate, both young men and women want friendship first and foremost and both mention love in equal numbers. In Haas's study, both young men and women want mates who are intelligent, funny, friendly, and lastly, good looking. Few choose mates primarily for sex.

E.J. Roberts discovered in his 1970s sex study of teenagers that only twelve parents in one hundred discuss sex with their children and only four in one hundred discuss contraception.[16] Only 9% of the girls and 11% of the boys Haas interviewed told their parents "everything." According to the survey, 71% of the boys and 74% of the girls told their parents "nothing at all," or at least "nothing that had anything to do with them."[17]

Sex researcher Michael Scofield found that teenagers who talked about sex with their parents were less likely to "do it" and less likely to be "anti-social."[18] What parents did not know could well hurt them (and their kids). It is not surprising, then, that teen films continue to insist that parents need to listen to their teenagers, and, ironically,

in the absence of such a dialogue—such is a conceit in the vast majority of teen movie narratives—the films themselves stand in with authoritative and authoritarian morality lessons of their own.

The Suspicion of Pleasure

The recent spate of American horror films depicting the punishment of promiscuous young women seems only an exaggerated consequence of the paternalistic and patriarchal reaction to the mythology of a sexual revolution. In *Halloween* (John Carpenter, 1978), the first and by far the best of these films, all the girls who "do it," "get it." The two teenagers of interest who survive—Laurie (the good girl) and Michael (the killer)—share one thing in common: they're both virgins.

In *Halloween, A Nightmare on Elm Street,* and *Friday the 13th* (Sean S. Cunningham, 1980), the central characters—the victims and potential victims—are young women. What is at stake in these films is not only the girls' sexuality, but an irrational, super (or sub) human violence that polices their desire, their chastity. In the wake of Kinsey and Masters and Johnson, one finds the bitterest of compensating values. The price of pleasure, of sexual freedom, is painfully high.

Halloween—and much the same can be said about *A Nightmare on Elm Street* and *Friday the 13th* and all of their sequels—tells us little about teenagers *per se*. Rather it focuses on the ignorance and neglect of their parents. For example, in *Halloween,* the police chief doesn't believe Michael will return. Michael does and kills the chief's daughter just as she is about to pick up her boyfriend to have sex. Michael attacks houses populated entirely by children and teenagers. Not a single parent is at home with their children (where they belong).

As such, *Halloween* chronicles a quintessential suburban nightmare. "Do you know what Haddonfield is?," the chief asks Michael's psychiatrist rhetorically, "families and houses all lined up in row . . . all lined up for slaughter." Unlike the everyday horrors faced by inner-city youths, for whom violence is at once real and natural, the suburban youths in these teen horror films face a terror that is supernatural and indestructible. Michael, for example, savagely kills his sister, then exits the house holding the bloody knife and waits pa-

tiently for his parents to return. His psychiatrist dispenses with any attempt to understand him. Instead, he refers to Michael as "the boogy man," as "pure evil." By the time Michael returns to Haddonfield "for revenge," he is a monster, a psychotic killer beyond reason and redemption.

Since horror films are about blame (for the invasion of "the other," in this case Michael), the teen horror variety rather predictably points to the teenagers' foundering parents. In *Halloween,* none of the parents listen to their kids. In *A Nightmare on Elm Street* and *Friday the 13th,* parents fail to tell their kids the truth until it's almost too late. Teenagers are invariably depicted spending virtually all of their time unsupervised, given ample motive and opportunity to do precisely what their parents say they don't want them to do. Since parents fail to enforce their authority, social regulation emerges magically, from elsewhere.

Carrie, another teen-horror picture, offers a variation on this theme regarding the discipline and punishment of sexually experienced youth. The film opens with a soft-focus, slow motion shower scene in the girls' locker room. As the camera pans Carrie's body, it first highlights her obliviousness to her own nakedness (as opposed to the rapture of her narcissistic classmates), then signals her sudden arrival into young adulthood as the blood of her first period drips down her leg. At the sight of her own blood, Carrie drops to the floor in abject fear. (Her mother has never told her there'd be days like this.) Her classmates ridicule her and toss tampons and sanitary napkins into the shower.

The teenagers in *Carrie* are a savage lot: cliqueish, narcissistic, and selfish. In the end, as their bodies are sent hurling against the walls of the gym on prom night, there is little doubt that they get what they deserve. Carrie on the other hand is an outsider, Cinderella in a school full of evil step sisters. She is, like Jim Stark in *Rebel Without a Cause,* alienated because she is good, terrorized by her classmates because she is different.

At home, Carrie's mother's insane religious fundamentalism is truly chilling, and Carrie's eventual refusal is, with all due respect to Hebdige, hardly oblique, but it is stylized. Her telekinetic powers (after all *Carrie* is based on a Stephen King story), are the physical mani-

> Scott: You didn't tell me it was a romance. I thought it was an action adventure flick.
> Norma: This is the movie we want to see, right girls?
> Susan: . . . and it's not exactly a romance. It's about the choices all women have to make.
> Scott: What choice is that? Whether to wear Calvin's or Levi's?
> Susan: No . . . it's the choice between love and independence. Between a man and a career.[26]

Susan's line of argument (above) suggests that for once it is the boys who are objectified, chosen or not chosen. But it also suggests that girls are making rather adult decisions long before boys have to take such things so seriously.

In "Jackie: An Ideology of Adolescent Femininity," Angela McRobbie argues that the romance and the teen-girl pulp magazines (like the U.K.'s *Jackie* and the U.S.'s *Seventeen*) isolate girls from each other, engendering a culture of treachery and deceit in the attempted acquisition of boys.[27] Barbara Bradby, in her study of the girl group sound of the early 1960s—for example, the Angels' "My Boyfriend's Back," the Chiffons' "He's So Fine," the Ronettes' "Be My Baby," and the Shangrilas' "Leader of the Pack"—shares McRobbie's suspicion of romance. "In the field of popular culture," Bradby posits, "romance has been the typically female manifestation of the imaginary. For women it represents a sphere of choice which can be opposed to the ending of choice in marriage, where the woman is symbolically chosen by the man." For married women, listening to popular music may be, like reading romances, an escapism which at the same time expresses dissatisfaction with their lot. But for teenagers, Bradby argues, the relationship between the symbolic and the imaginary is reversed; they live for real what for others is a fantasy world, denoting a social space "in-between the patriarchal control of parents and the symbolic order of marriage."[28]

Nostalgia and Romance

As one Iowa teenager puts it, "I call (it) a romance because she doesn't know she is falling in love."[29] The problem is, as most adults see it, teenagers are always convinced they are falling in love.

The premise that teenagers take themselves far too seriously resides at the heart of the *Beach Party* films of the early sixties, movies that celebrate, as William Asher, the director of *Beach Party* puts it, "good clean sex."[30] The *Beach Party* films so trivialize youth that it is hard to believe anyone ever took them seriously. And perhaps that was their point: that this deadly seriousness with which teenagers generally take their lives could well be a source of amusement for those older at heart. Released over a decade later and directed at a similar audience, *Grease* (Randal Kleiser, 1978) gently pokes fun at the *Beach Party* films, as if they actually were artifacts of anyone's real-life past, as if they are artifacts of a once-lived innocence lost forever. The film splits Gidget's (that is girl + midget = gidget) and Annette's socio-sexual crisis into two characters: Rizzo, a tough girl with a heart of gold, and Sandy, a bland and blond "good" girl. In an early scene, Rizzo dons a blonde wig (mocking Sandy) and sings: "Look at me/I'm Sandra Dee [the original Gidget]/Lousy with virginity/Won't go to bed 'til I'm legally wed/I can't/I'm Sandra Dee!" Later on, she sings: "There are worse things I could do/Than go with a boy or two." Though Rizzo indeed "goes all the way," the song assures us, at least she's not a tease like Sandy, Annette, and Gidget.

Grease, like *Beach Party* and *Where the Boys Are,* focuses on girl subculture soley with regard to sexuality and posits that girls are punished no matter what they do. For example, in *Grease,* when Rizzo sings about Sandra Dee, she is at an all-girls slumber party in a friend's bedroom, seated, like a proper teeny-bopper, under posters of Troy Donahue and Elvis. When, in song, she chronicles her sexual misadventures, she is outside and all alone. Her drama, and these are the stakes for girls, consistently regards her relationship to the bedroom. And her rite of passage into womanhood carries with it the very threat of pregnancy that formalizes the reality of sexual difference.

But such seriousness is put aside in the romantic comedy ending of the film. Sandy arrives at the graduation carnival in skin-tight leather, hair teased, smoking (and coughing), talking tough, and apparently ready for action. Danny, her greaser paramour, is wearing his letterman's sweater and his hair is poofed (as opposed to slicked-back). Despite the drama that otherwise characterized this, their final

71

year in high school, the kids are, in the end, all right. Sandy and Danny reaffirm their relationship. Rizzo announces that she isn't pregnant after all, and her (relieved) boyfriend vows to stick by her anyway. The beauty-school dropout—thanks to her teen angel played by Frankie Avalon—is back on track. The rest of the school comes together as one to celebrate the superficiality of difference.

As these happy teenagers sing and dance out of the frame and into adulthood, they rather affirm their essential conformity. Difference, all along, had just been a matter or style. And contrary to Hebdige's convincing argument,[31] style is at once fleeting and superficial. *Grease* ultimately argues that no matter who you are—greaser, preppy, good girl, bad girl—you can always be assimilated into something/someone else.

It's Just Sex

In *Fast Times at Ridgemont High* (1983), a film about teenage girls directed by a woman, Amy Heckerling, we find the sexual rite of passage into womanhood staged with seriousness, sensitivity, and honesty. While films mythologizing boys' "first time" range from the puerile (*Porky's* [Bob Clark, 1982] and *The Last American Virgin* [Boaz Davidson, 1982]) to the romantic (*Say Anything* [Cameron Crowe, 1989] and *The Summer of '42* [Robert Mulligan, 1971]), *Fast Times at Ridgemont High* is, despite its helter-skelter pace and light-comedic tone, starkly realistic when it comes to teen sex.[32]

Stacy, the film's young heroine, is (still!) a virgin. With the help of a friend, the far more experienced Linda, she remedies the situation in short order. In most teen films about boys losing their virginity the big event is saved for the end; the rest of the film exists as no more than a tease. In *Fast Times at Ridgemont High,* Stacy's first experience is the catalyst that sets the narrative in motion.[33]

At the beginning of the film, we see Stacy at work at the pizza parlor in the mall. There, she flirts with Ron, a salesman at the stereo store. Though she can hardly believe her newfound courage, she gives him her number. But, alas, several days go by and he doesn't call. "Call him," her friend Linda urges. But Stacy is still too self-conscious. "Guys love that sort of thing," Linda adds, "What are you

waiting for? You're sixteen years old! I did it when I was thirteen. It's no huge thing. It's just sex.''

When Stacy and Ron finally get together, they end up in the dugout at an abandoned baseball field. Stacy tells him she's nineteen. He says he's twenty-six. Both lies are equally ridiculous. We hear, "She's Gonna Be Somebody's Baby," on the soundtrack, but the sex is hardly so romantic. She is somebody's baby, all right, but not as the song intends. The film makes it abundantly clear that she is still a child.

What makes the scene cinematically interesting is that it is shot entirely from her point of view. While they are having sex, we see in his face his total self-absorption. We share her view of the ceiling. And we realize just how emotionally disconnected she is. The scene is not romantic, but it is not ruinous either. Rather, it's anti-climactic, ironic, embarrassing.

Later, when Ron fails to call back, Linda places the entire episode in what she thinks is its proper context. "What do you care?," she quips, "He's a stereo salesman. What did you want to do? Marry him? Have kids with him? It's his loss." Later in the film, when her eventual boyfriend Mark doesn't come across even after Stacy throws herself at him, Linda provides more such status-conscious advice. "What do you care about Mark Rattner? He's an usher at the movie theater. You work in the best food stand in the mall."

Though Linda pays for such hard-hearted advice in the end of the film when she receives a Dear Jane letter from her much older boyfriend, Stacy's search for her sexual self is painful throughout. When she seduces Mark's best friend Damone, we again hear "She's Gonna Be Somebody's Baby" on the soundtrack. Like the first time, the act itself is anti-climactic. He ejaculates almost immediately, then whines, "I think I came. Did you feel it?" "I guess I did," she responds. When he exits, humiliated, we see her, bored, confused, and totally naked.

Stacy's humiliation is highlighted the following day as Damone refuses to make eye contact with her at school. When she discovers that she's pregnant, he coldly remarks: "It was your idea. You wanted it more than I did." But Stacy stands her ground. She tells him that she plans to have an abortion, that he should pay half and give her a ride to the clinic.

But when Damone tries to assemble the funds, he fails to get any money at all. In such a time of crisis, he is no longer such a big operator; he's just a teenager in a bind. The next morning we see him forlorn, seated under two posters in his bedroom; one is of Who guitarist Peter Townshend, his head down in his bloody right hand, the other is of Elvis Costello, in close-up, glowering at the camera under a single word title, "trust."

When it's time to go to the clinic, Damone stands Stacy up. She is forced to bum a ride from her brother, and though she tries to trick him, he discovers the awful truth. Throughout, Heckerling refuses to trivialize or romanticize teen sex, just as she refuses to eroticize Stacy's nudity.

The boys in the film are a ridiculous bunch. Mark, the one reasonably good kid, is overwhelmed by the whole dating scene. Though he and Stacy end up together in the end—we are told in the final titles that they are happy but "still have not gone all the way"—he is not much to look at or to talk with. Damone is a conceited jerk. Stacy's brother, Brad, is introduced washing his car to the tune of "I'm an All-American Boy." His life revolves around a series of demeaning jobs: at All-American Burger, at Captain Hook's Fish and Chips, and at the Mi-T-Mat convenience store. Though he claims to be "a single, successful guy," his girlfriend dumps him to go out with other boys, he gets fired from two of the three jobs, ends up the manager at the Mi-T-Mart for the foreseeable future, and gets caught masturbating by Linda. Spicolli, a drugged-out surfer offers ample comic relief but clings to the puerile fantasies he reads in *Playboy* and *Penthouse*.

At the end of *Fast Times at Ridgemont High*, Stacy tells Linda, "I finally figured out what I want. I don't want sex. I want a relationship. I want romance." What Stacy learns is that she wasn't ready, that Mark's reluctance to take advantage of her (or to let her take advantage of him) was the best thing that happened to her so far in high school.

In *Hollywood from Vietnam to Reagan*, Robin Wood concludes that *Fast Times at Ridgemont High*'s "treatment of adolescent sexuality is consistently enlightened and intelligent," which he connects with the fact that the film was directed by a woman. For Wood, the woman's point of view subverts the ideological function of virtually all other

teen films (for Wood, a compliance to and participation in "what are essentially male rituals of desire and guilt"). According to Wood— and this is an argument he posits with regard to nearly every seventies' and eighties' film, from *Fast Times at Ridgemont High* to *Raging Bull* (Martin Scorsese, 1980)—such an ideology regards a trenchant homophobia. The obsessive emphasis on "getting laid" in teen movies, for example, "can be seen as an unconscious acknowledgment of the reality of the threat" of one's own gay feelings. For Wood, the raging machismo of contemporary Hollywood cinema regards the reality of teenage boys' (and the overgrown teenage boys who run the studios') fear of their own homosexual fantasies and desires.[34]

In an interesting footnote to his discussion of *Fast Times at Ridgemont High,* Wood briefly discusses *Revenge of the Nerds* (Jeff Kanew, 1984), a recent teen film that features a disarming, comical gay black college student. *Revenge of the Nerds* is at once a formulaic and sophomoric take on an already formulaic and sophomoric teen film, *Animal House* (John Landis, 1978), though instead of the glamorous sixties' hedonists of Delta House, we instead have a group of unpopular geeks, all of whom are reviled because they are not only good students but they are actually interested in school.[36]

But like *Fast Times at Ridgemont High, Revenge of the Nerds* glibly critiques the conventional teen romance. In a particularly funny scene in *Revenge of the Nerds,* a nerd gets his big chance with the campus's most desirable coed, and he makes the most of his opportunity. Out of breath after a satisfying bit of lovemaking—and this is juxtaposed to her unsatisfying encounters with desirable campus studs—she asks if all nerds are "that good." "Sure," he responds, "We have to be. We're nerds. We're grateful."

Charting the Sexual Wilderness

When, in 1966, Packard interviewed young women at New York University, one coed remarked: "I actually think young people are pushed into sex today because of what they see on television, in the movies and what Madison Avenue promotes."[37] This is clearly what Packard wanted to hear, but the evidence (of such encouragement) just isn't there in the teen film. The most exploitative films about

teen sex—the wild youth and horror pictures—end up disastrously for promiscuous youth. The mild youth beach films, despite being sexist, are hardly sexy. Television shows like *Father Knows Best, The Ozzie and Harriet Show, Happy Days, Room 222, Square Pegs, Beverly Hills 90210, Fame, The White Shadow, Eight is Enough, Family,* and *My Two Dads,* to name just a few, never reward extramarital sex. If it happens at all—and it generally doesn't—everybody's so sorry they don't know where or how to begin to tell us. Even films like *Where the Boys Are* and *Fast Times at Ridgemont High,* which focus on the moral and ethical implications of teen sex, encourage female teens to wait. One can hardly find more convincing spokespersons for abstinence than Melanie and Stacy.

Teenagers have sex, or don't have sex, for a multitude of reasons—reasons which sometimes make sense and sometimes don't, and often are so intrinsic to the culture of youth as to be incomprehensible to those of us on the outside looking in. At times, and this seems to me an apt conclusion here, things don't even make sense to the principles involved, evidenced in the following confessional made by Holden Caulfield in *The Catcher in the Rye*: "Last year I made a rule that I was going to quit horsing around with girls that, deep down, gave me a pain in the ass. I broke it, though, the same week I made it—the same night as a matter of fact. I spent the whole night necking with a terrible phoney named Anne Louise Sherman. Sex is something I just don't understand. I swear to God I don't."[38]

Chapter 4

The Struggle for Fun

The politics of consumption dominates the critical literature attending to youth culture. But as discussed in the introduction, there is hardly a consensus on the subject. In studies conducted just after the Second World War the "culture industry" model prevails; youth is seen as the product of mass media manipulation, coercion, and market strategy. More recently, the notion of cause and effect has been problematized; the concept of youth as at once a mass movement and a mass market has fostered a view of youth's autonomy within and despite the marketplace.

In "The Young Audience," an example of the contemporary approach, Stuart Hall and Paddy Whannel insist on "the active participation of the younger generation in their own subculture," promoting the view of youth culture as "a spontaneous and generative response to a frequently bewildering and confused social situation."[1] While accounting for the media's tendency to appropriate and thus re-define and dilute youth culture (its "colonization" of the cultural and ideological sphere), Hall and Whannel extol youth's spontaneity, its autonomy.

Such an optimistic and progressive account is shared by Dick Hebdige in *Subculture: The Meaning of Style*. Hebdige argues that youth's recourse to the materials and materiality of style, its spectacularization of everyday objects, speech, fashion, and music (i.e. its encoded representations of opposition in and through material culture), evinces "a symbolic violation of the social order," a serious challenge to cultural hegemony. Post-World War II youth, according to Hebdige, at once redefined (denoting a "secret meaning" to) and found themselves defined by their stylistic appropriation of such everyday objects

by the conscripts, and exploitation of themselves by the crafty little absolute beginners."[7] For MacInnes, making it through adolescence involves an ongoing series of consumerist temptations, each one attending to an erosion of no longer vital, innocent youth culture.

All the principal characters in the novel change; they grow up. In doing so, they also take a turn for the worse. Dean Swift, for example, the novel's ever so cool "modern jazz creation," succumbs to drug addiction and sells his image of dispassionate, hip youth in the unnamed narrators' photographs. The Fabulous Hoplite, Soho's "low rent Oscar Wilde," rebels against the macho heterosexuality of mainstream adult and youth culture, but, like Swift, he too allows himself to become a commodity, an image in the prurience of masturbatory fantasy. Both sell out and turn unapologetically cynical and hedonistic. At the end of the novel, both await chronological adulthood, already old beyond their years.

Though it is partially a structural conceit, MacInnes's narrator stands outside the faddish youth and staid adult cultures. While all those around him acquiesce to the material world, and, as the novel has it, grow up too fast, the narrator finds himself caught in a fascinating and complex narrative fix. He can either sell-out and curtail his teen freedom, or, perhaps worse yet, resist temptation, exploitation, commodification and become as naive and pathetic as Peter Pan, the victim of the fantasy of remaining forever young, the very thing he so ardently critiques throughout the course of the novel.

Because of such a narrative fix, the narrator, like Holden Caulfield in *The Catcher in the Rye,* gets hopelessly lost. At the end of the novel, we find him at the airport welcoming black Africans to "have a ball" in racist, violent London, sort of planning to go to either Oslo or Buenos Aires, but it doesn't much matter which. He too has become hopelessly cynical, perhaps even mad.

At the end of *The Catcher in the Rye,* Caulfield is "damn near bawling"[8] watching his little sister go around and around on a Merry-go-Round. His refusal or inability to fit in with his peers or with the adult world he so convincingly derides as patently phoney, leads to an incapacitating nervous breakdown. The novel, though widely read as a celebration of the alienated teen, ends in regret and the hero's pathetic promise of conformity.

While Salinger's fiction ends in the solitude of insanity, perhaps positing "much madness as divinest sense,"[9] MacInnes prophesizes a far uglier scenario. His narrator displays a love-hate relationship with "that old whore London," come to life in the hands and hearts and minds of the "kiddoes." But while youth seems to rise, phoenix-like, from the ashes of the fallen Empire, the newborn or reborn communal pride leads to the revival of European fascism. Such a frightening move to the right is offered as the logical extension of youth's search for authority, its search for identity, fidelity, and community in a culture gone static or just gone bad.

In *Pop Songs and Teenagers,* MacInnes notes that it would be "possible to see, in the teenage neutralism and indifference to politics, and self-sufficiency, and instinct for enjoyment—in short their kind of happy mindlessness—the raw material for crypto-fascisms of the worst kind."[10] In *Absolute Beginners,* all the teenagers, including the novel's narrator, are apolitical. And though the narrator resists the temptation (and thus ends up all alone), most of his peers fall prey to the seductive rhetoric of neo-Nazism.

From the start, the narrator distances himself from conventional, contemporary politics. For example, early on in the novel, he tells Mickey Ponderoso (initials M.P.—a representative of conservative, adult England): "No one under twenty is interested in that bomb of yours one little bit."[11] Later, when Ponderoso starts in talking about the queen, the narrator bristles, "that's a subject we're very, very tired of."[12]

The (real) race riots of 1958, which MacInnes attributed to teen aimlessness, apolitics, and impatience, also smacked of youth's perverse attraction to conformity. Early on in the novel, MacInnes makes this point through Dean Swift. "These teenagers are ceasing to be rational, thinking human beings," Swift muses, "they're turning into mindless butterflies all of the same size and colour, that have to flutter round exactly the same flowers, in exactly the same gardens."[13]

Though they are depicted as at once aimless and conformist, when push comes to shove—indeed, it is two prams colliding head on, neither "mum" willing to step aside that starts the fray—youth resorts to violence, falling headlong into the maximum entropy of chaos and riot. But in the very act of riot, and MacInnes is smart to lay it out

this way, youth makes the transition to adulthood, affirming their adoption of the very culture they had theretofore rejected.

Julian Temple's 1986 film adaptation of the novel was coincidentally released to headlines heralding a second wave of race riots in Great Britain. On a first look, the film is just a buoyant, jubilant musical, fraught with references to *Love Me Tonight* (Rouben Mamoulian, 1932), *An American in Paris* (Vincente Minnelli, 1951), *West Side Story* (Robert Wise, 1961), and especially *One From the Heart* (Francis Coppola, 1982). Like his more recent *Earth Girls Are Easy* (1988), *Absolute Beginners* is a *tour de force* of steadicam cinematography and pop postmodernism. A closer look, though, reveals a rationale for such stylistic indulgence (and such a departure from the novel), as the film faithfully attends to the spirit if not the letter of MacInnes' dour parable regarding the wages of fun in youth's search for authority.

The film's only real "problem" is that Temple is constrained by the generic formula of the movie musical: boy meets girl, boy loses girl, boy gets girl. In the novel—and this is the most telling difference between the two *Absolute Beginners*—the narrator rescues Crepe Suzette (his heart's desire) from (her husband of convenience) Henley during the climactic teen riots and takes her back to his flat. Just as they are about to finally have sex, his half-brother Vern bursts in with news that his father, who is about to die, is asking for him. Faced with such a moral dilemma, the narrator sends Vern away and decides to remain with Suzette. Though getting the girl and finally losing his virginity should mark some sort of significant rite of passage, instead it signals yet another wrong choice made by a teenager in a moment of moral crisis.

The entire novel, like the film, is a tease for this scene. But, as with any other commodity gotten in the novel, it is at best bittersweet. "There in my place in Napoli," he laments, "we made it at last, but honest, you couldn't say it was sexy—it was just love."[14] In the film, we see "Colin" (MacInnes's unnamed narrator) and Suzette make love as the final credits roll. As the title song plays we celebrate his loss of virginity. He's no longer an absolute beginner, on that level at least.

What the novel and film share is a sincere warning regarding Britain's steady move to the right; no matter that the narrator claims he

doesn't care about politics, in the end he must make a choice. He does, but it does him no good. Though he sympathizes with the blacks, indeed it is their culture he best likes, because he's white his attempt to join them backfires. Guilty by association—for being a white teen-ager—Colin is chased down an alley by a gang of angry young blacks. There he is saved by "the Wiz," his best friend at the start of the narrative, a petty grifter gone pimp gone racist thug who invites Colin to "come to the real teenage ball." He does, and finds himself at a White Defence League rally, where we and he listen to the sloganized, reductive politics of hate: "We don't want the blacks or Jews, yellow red, black and blue. Let's get rid of the homos too. Fascism is here to stay. Trains on time, regular pay. Jobs for all the Christian whites. Hate's the way to win our fight. Hate's the way we will unite."

When Colin appears unimpressed, the Wiz puts it on the line: "What's it gonna be, teenager?" That the messages are all hardly subtle is the point here. Colin rejects Wiz's fascist cronies and is rewarded (in the film) as he and Suzette finally "make it" at his place in Napoli. And consistent with the musical-comedy happy ending, in a pointed reversal of history clearly not lost on the British audience, we see the riot give way to a street festival celebrating interracial harmony.

But despite such a happy ending, a rather more paradoxical subtext emerges. By realizing his adolescent dreams, in the very act of "get-ting" Crepe Suzette, Colin repudiates the lunatic violence of youth. It is at least ironic that in a film that so spectacularizes youth culture, closure rather firmly rejects such a culture as fleeting, cynical, fascist, racist, and self-destructive. At the end, what is being celebrated is Colin and Suzette's adulthood.

Disposable Income/Disposable Youth

The culture of conformity and consumerism hit its pinnacle—or its nadir, depending on how you look at it—in the early sixties in London with the mod phenomenon. As Simon Frith describes them: "the mods were arrogant and narcissistic, cynical and tense; they came on like winners and consumption was, for them, as much a playground and a last resort; the urge was movement—from shop to shop, club to club—

speeding on pills, on dance floors, on the latest fashion coup."[15] Indeed, as one mod put it in an interview in the early sixties: "When you were at work, you were a nobody. So when you put on your suede or mohair suit and desert boots and go to the dancehall, you want to be somebody to your mates . . . You make a statement through your clothes, or your dancing, or your scooter. You had to be cool."[16]

The notion of the dance floor as a stage resurfaced in the American disco craze. Movies like *Saturday Night Fever* (John Badham, 1977) and *Thank God It's Friday* (Robert Klane, 1978), counterpoint the boredom of dead-end day jobs with the furtive glory of success on the dance floor. Donna Summer, the Bee Gees, and K.C. and the Sunshine Band all extolled the virtues of leisure and conspicuous consumption as one's entitlement after a week's exploitation on the job. "Disco was about eroticism and ecstasy as material goods," Simon Frith argues, "the disco experience revealed the artificiality and transcience of your feelings—they were produced to be consumed; and disco pleasure, as it moved into the consumer mainstream, became the pleasure of consumption itself."[17]

Such a politics of consumption similarly epitomized the mod subculture. As Hebdige suggests, the mods exhibited the very essence of his theory of "stylistic generation," the very "meaning of style." The mods borrowed from the world of adult consumer commodities and then transcribed the meaning of these objects with subcultural rather than dominant cultural values. "[The mods] seemed to consciously invert," he argues, "the values associated with smart dress, to deliberately challenge the assumptions, to falsify the expectations derived from such sources."[18] Hebdige further argues that the mods raised consumption to a "new level"—a sort of fetishizing of style. In such a practice, the mods embodied how subcultures live "their real situation" as "an imaginary relation."[19]

Hebdige unsurprisingly finds the mod style wholly progressive. He views their style, their look as "a parody of the consumer society in which they [were] situated."[20] According to Hebdige, the mods' clean-cut look—their embodiment of the very *image* of youth cherished by their parents and employers—was a cynical and sardonic undermining of the importance of appearance to adults (just as it coordinated the importance of appearance to them). The mods reclaimed the clean-

cut look as their own, deliberately juxtaposing a conservative appearance to a hardly conservative lifestyle.

Much like the British punks who emerged over a decade later, the
mods copped a purely referential style, citing: the American movie
mafioso and Brooklyn "sharp-kid"; the British wartime black-mar-
keteer, the "wide boy"; the Jamaican hustler and the dissolute scions
of the trendy West End/Chelsea jet set.[21] In each allusion and transformation—if we are to buy Hebdige's semiotic model—the mod embodied a critique of a whole series of media and mediated images
originating from outside their own rather limited experience. The
gangster, the black, and the white jet-setter coalesced as the commodity (itself) became (their) culture.

At the heart of both the disco and mod experience was a formal
split between day and night, work and play. Neither subculture en-
tertained patently false dreams of social mobility and "success" in
the workplace—hence the gangster and idle rich role models. The
compensation for a relatively low status in one world was the easy
purchase of an elevated status in another (in the dance hall and on
the streets).

With modest disposable incomes, both groups curtailed adolescence
in a hurry. Entering the work world while likely still living at home
with their parents, the mods and disco faddists placed a priority on
immediate and transitory gratification. Displaying an astounding
stamina—after all, they were living a double life—both subcultures
reveled in the false satisfactions provided for them by the culture
industry. Indeed, they reveled in knowing that such satisfactions are
false.

Still, at the core of it all was a lot of fun, as evidenced in the
following itinerary laid out by "a typical mod" in an interview published in the Sunday London *Times* in April, 1964:

> Monday night meant dancing at the Mecca, the Hammersmith Pa-
> lais, the Purley Orchard, or the Streatham Locarno. Tuesday meant
> Soho and the Scene Club. Wednesday was Marquee night. Thursday
> was reserved for the ritual washing of the hair. Friday meant the
> Scene again. Saturday afternoon usually meant shopping for clothes
> and records. Saturday night was spent dancing and rarely finished
> before 9:00 or 10:00 Sunday morning. Sunday night meant the Flam-

ingo or, perhaps, if one showed signs of weakening, could be spent sleeping.

Such a priority on play and its opposition to the work-a-day world is aptly captured in *Quadrophenia* (Franc Roddam, 1979), a film based loosely on (the former mod band) the Who's rock opera of the same name. The film presents a series of episodes of teens making out, fighting with rival gangs, listening to music, dancing, scoring and doing drugs, hanging out, feuding with siblings and parents, masturbating, vandalizing property and running away from home—in other words, a realistic account, at the high-speed pace of the mod, of teen life.

Apropos the mod lifestyle, the first fifty minutes of the film takes place at nighttime, and virtually every scene is a crowd. When it is finally daytime, we see Jimmy, the film's hero, at work as a mail-boy at a posh advertising firm. Surrounded by images of inaccessible women and wealth, Jimmy finds the whole work scene debasing and alienating. Eventually, though, Jimmy does enjoy a daylit triumph. But it too ends up an alienating experience. While on holiday in Brighton, Jimmy joins the sea of green parkas and white scooters, chanting: "We are the mods, we are the mods, we are, we are, we are the mods." As he and his subculture mark their tenuous solidarity, they rather dramatically transform the one-time Victorian seaside retreat. For him and his mates, it is not only a moment of transcendence, it is a moment of sweet revenge.

Fidelity and diversity, belongingness and independence, conformity and originality are all regarded in the film as the central paradoxes of the mod experience. When Jimmy and a childhood friend meet and discover that they belong to rival teen factions—Jimmy's a mod; his friend, a rocker—they argue the relative merits of their subcultures. "I don't want to be the same as everybody else," Jimmy says, "that's why I'm a mod." To add irony to an already ironic remark, the rocker adds: "That's why I joined the army—to be different."

Such a conformity, though, coalesced for the mods in the form of a profound generational solidarity—hence the mod anthem, "My Generation." The specific look, the dances, the dating rituals, the scooters, and the music that documented and defined their world suggested that if you shopped at the right stores, danced the proper steps,

"pulled the smart birds," drove an Italian scooter, and listened to the appropriate bands you were OK. For the mods, fashion became an end in itself.

In *Quadrophenia,* Jimmy ably follows such a fashion, embracing the hell-bent hedonism with a kind of desperate fervor. But at the end, he cannot escape his fundamental difference from the maddening crowd. For that refusal—after all he is the film's only hero—he pays a big price.

Jimmy's eventual, inevitable repudiation of the mod lifestyle—and his youth as well—begins with an ill-fated romance with the film's teen *femme fatale,* Steph, the object of his desire and perhaps the motivation behind his affiliation with the mods. He first captures Steph's attention before the road trip to Brighton after he burglarizes a pharmacy and then generously shares his drugs with her. Though she heads to Brighton on the back of a friend's scooter, she soon pays him back. Caught up in the excitement of the riots, she dumps her escort. Jimmy seizes the day—or more accurately, she does—and they retreat to a back alley and have sex.

When they return to the fray, Jimmy is nabbed by the police. Following his day in court and night in jail, Jimmy returns to find Steph arm in arm with his (ex)best friend. "Brighton was just a giggle," she tells him, "That's all. I fancied you. It didn't mean anything." Shattered by such a heartless rejection, Jimmy mounts his scooter, drives recklessly, and gets hit broadside by a milktruck. When the driver exits the truck, Jimmy shouts: "You killed my scooter!" It is clear that some part of him, of his identity as a mod, is destroyed.

The film ends with a protracted journey to the White Cliffs of Dover as we hear virtually all of side four of the Who album in the back-ground. As the refrain of "Love Reign O'er Me" lists all the things Jimmy has "had enough of," we see the scooter he has robbed from the Mod leader "the Ace Face" plummet into the sea. But we do not see Jimmy. Whether or not he dies, we gather, is less important than the symbolic end of his youth and the symbolic rejection of the seemingly anarchic mod lifestyle.

The Commodity Becomes the Culture

Much moreso than any other band, the Beatles came to epitomize swinging London in the 1960s. Indeed, their frivolity, their "chirpy optimism," rendered absurd any question of youth's entitlement.

The Beatles' ability to forge "a politics of optimism,"[23] is well captured in their debut on screen, *A Hard Day's Night* (Richard Lester, 1964), a film that proclaimed the triumph of youthful exuberance over a stodgy older generation and a relentless domestic economic collapse. *A Hard Day's Night* depicts the band members as cheerful, amiable youths, mugging interviews, sneaking out to go to dance-parties, fooling and manipulating their parent-like managers, playing music because for them it was easy and fun. For example, when Ringo gets (just a little) down, John leads the band in an acoustic version of "This Boy," and Ringo is quickly cured. Earlier on, aboard Brit-Rail, John says "let's do something," and, as if they were in a Judy Garland/Mickey Rooney picture, the boys decide to put on a show. As for their subcultural affiliation, they have none—they are about in-(rather than ex-)clusion. When Ringo is asked if he's a mod or a rocker, he answers diplomatically: "I'm neither. I'm a mocker."

Like *Absolute Beginners*, *A Hard Day's Night* is stylistically hectic. Richard Lester, the film's director, was, by 1964, an experienced producer of television commercials. Such experience paid off, as it was Lester's ability to reduce the appeal of the Beatles to a series of brief vignettes and to engage and mix and match a plethora of styles (from television, surrealism, *cinema verité*, and slapstick comedy) that so ably signaled the universality and versatility of the Beatles. It also allowed Lester to herald the Beatles' stardom. Indeed every shot refers to such an obvious fact.

For example, when we see the Beatles do their live television spot, Lester intercuts shots of the hysterical schoolgirls in jittery close-up with very un-television-like low angle shots of the stars on stage. Cinematically, Lester encourages the audience to fall in love with the ways in which the Beatles are unlike them.

From the very outset of the film, we see the Beatles reproduced in photographs, an ongoing theme highlighted by the film's cut-up look. What we gain access to is a Beatles' (filmic) scrapbook, a collection of images that define our role as fans, as consumers of their stardom.

When we hear their music on the soundtrack, we often see the band play-acting, not even lip-synching their songs. Their freedom is at once an ideal and an idealism we watch from a distance. The handheld camera style utilized in these scenes alludes to direct cin-

ema, an American documentary form that often examined the real lives of bigger-than-life stars (e.g. *Don't Look Back* [D.A. Pennebaker, 1967] and *Gimme Shelter* [David and Albert Maysles, 1970]). But the effect in *A Hard Day's Night* is completely the opposite. Lester's evocation of the direct cinema style suggests that any attempt to "capture" the Beatles is futile. They move too fast. And they have no "real" life. Their inaccessibility is held up as the logical extension of stardom: the scrapbook of images is as close to them as we will ever get. Stylistically, Lester demystifies stardom; thematically he glorifies it. Ultimately, the ease and fun of the Beatles is regarded as an ideal, a counterpoint to the hysteria of their fans and a generation born to follow.

While the film features an early example of the now commonplace pop music package—indeed, the film is a very long commercial for the Beatles' records—*A Hard Day's Night* narrativizes an arch critique of the merchandising of youth. In a particularly funny vignette, George happens in on an advertising agency specializing in youth-oriented products. There he meets an executive who speaks derisively about teenagers. "They're fab and all those other pimply hyperboles," he says. But when he shows George the new shirts he plans to market, George responds curtly: "They're grotty [grotesque]." The executive notes the word "grotty" for Susan, the agency's "real trend setter" (who George finds "a drag"), but otherwise dismisses George and his "utterly valueless opinions." "The new thing," he bristles, "is to care passionately and to be right wing." However accurate he is on that score, George's bemused exit signals that his, like the rest of the Beatles', popularity is no trend. Those who follow him know the real thing when they see it.

The Culture Becomes the Commodity

In 1964, the year *A Hard Day's Night* was released, two Chicago businessmen bought a pillowcase that one of the Beatles slept on from a local hotel for $1,000. They then cut the pillowcase into 160,000 one-square-inch pieces and sold them for $1.00 each. In that same year, the Beatles' success enabled (their British record company) EMI's profits to rise 80%. From 1964–1969, roughly from *A Hard*

Day's Night to the break-up of the band, in the United States the Beatles accounted for more than 50% of Capitol Records' profits. As late as 1973, over three years after the band had called it quits, the sale of Beatles' anthologies still accounted for 28.6% of EMI's profits.[24] In the black and white of such impressive statistics, youth culture, *vis à vis* the Beatles, had become a commodity.

Preceding the release of *A Hard Day's Night* by about a year, *Bye Bye Birdie* (George Sidney, 1963) purposefully trivialized the very formidable pop/rock youth culture the Beatles had begun to coalesce. Loosely based on the drafting of Elvis Presley into the U.S. Army, *Bye Bye Birdie* catalogues and, like the fifties' films of Frank Tashlin and scenarios of George Axelrod, gently lampoons the strained seriousness of such postwar phenomena as the Cold War, the space race, the population explosion, television, and rock and roll youth culture. The central comic figure in the film is the pop-star himself, Conrad Birdie, played by Jesse Pearson as an oversized and oversexed narcissist with a girlish walk and a glass jaw. Pearson's performance effectively satirized Elvis's quintessential fifties' machismo just as it eerily foreshadowed Elvis's future, fatso Las Vegas style.

Bye Bye Birdie, much like *The Girl Can't Help It* (Frank Tashlin, 1956), rather hedges its bet on youth culture. The film co-stars appealing adults Dick Van Dyke, Janet Leigh, Paul Lynde, and Maureen Stapleton along with pop-star Bobby Rydell and the then-teenage Ann-Margret as every boy's dream. The music is tame; the dances, choreographed by Gower Champion, hardly suggest how teenagers in America were beginning to use dance as a kind of public sexual ritual. Despite alluding to Elvis and the rock culture that formed in his wake, *Bye Bye Birdie* insists that youth culture is more than a little bit ridiculous, and that Elvis's aggressive sexuality that had so wowed teenage consumers was little more than a cover for a glass jaw.

Indicatively, the film ends with Birdie in disgrace and the kids scurrying to get pinned and grow up like their parents. The teenagers and their parents got all worked up over nothing. *Bye Bye Birdie* concludes much as its best-known production number does, with the ironic sentiment that "Nothing's the matter with kids today!"

Fascism and Consumerism

A far less comic turn on the rock and roll culture industry emerges in 1967 with Peter Watkins's dour futurist pseudo-documentary *Privilege*. Watkins's film owes much to *A Hard Day's Night*, but it refuses to accept the myth of the transcendent star: the notion that charismatic stars, like the Beatles, somehow stand outside and above the vertically integrated marketing scheme that delivers their image and sound. Both films cop the aesthetics of sixties' ciné-realism, but while Lester uses technique to insist that what's behind the scenes isn't nearly as important as what we see on stage or hear on record, Watkins insists that the real drama is in the boardroom and the star is at once inconsequent and rather easily replaced.

Privilege opens with fictive rock star Stephen Shorter (played by then real rock star Paul Jones) on stage, hands secured in cuffs behind his back, jailed, released, and eventually beaten by brutal uniformed guards. His music is dominated by theatrics just as the Beatles is not. And while Watkins inserts shots of Shorter's female fans in the throes of teenage erotic bliss, the context of these shots denotes the disconnectedness of Shorter's performance from their reaction. From the start we know that something's askew.

After the performance, we tour one of the many Stephen Shorter Discotheques. The products on sale there all bear the S.S. emblem, an early and ironic reference to rock and roll fascism. The advertising slogan for the merchandise is no less pernicious: "When you are buying here, you are buying Stephen Shorter."

Shorter's management team is hardly the bumbling bunch depicted in *A Hard Day's Night*. Instead, Stephen Shorter Enterprises is overseen by the director of the Merchants Bank. Shorter's entourage of hangers-on and publicity managers and music arrangers are comic only because they are so unself-conscious. From the start it is clear they are only along for the ride.

When Shorter's management team decides to change Shorter's image, the "star" is brought in only after the fact. We discover along with Shorter that he was made to *appear* more violent than any other pop star so that, when the time was right, he could be made to repent.

As the team gears up for Shorter's transformation, consultants are brought in to design clothing and revamp the musical arrangements, all without the star's consent.

Shorter is again excluded when the team discusses corporate sponsorship for the upcoming tour (then unheard of, but now commonplace on the rock scene). Choosing from several different candidates, the board agrees on the Interfaith Council who plan to use Shorter's ritual/symbolic act of contrition to bolster faltering church attendance. In the climactic scene of the film, Shorter becomes the poster boy for Christian Crusade Week. Decked out in papal red togs, he is told to lead his followers "to a better way of life—a fruitful conformity."

The new look tour is supported by two hit songs: the first by Shorter himself, featuring the lyrics: "Forgive me please/I'm down on my knees/I've been a bad bad boy"; the second, by his back-up band, an upbeat version of "Onward Christian Soldiers." The inaugural concert is staged just like Leni Riefenstahl's *Triumph of the Will* (1935). It is an unapologetic, unironic spectacle of nationalism as religion, as corporate might, as fascism. The scene is set in the National Stadium and begins as a little altar boy offers the opening address. This first invocation of religion is followed by marching bands, youth scouts in uniform carrying flags, the lighting of a fiery cross, soldiers firing cannons, the lighting of yet another fiery cross, and a procession of Christian clergy entering the field to the strains of Handel's "Messiah." "What you are seeing," the documentary (voice-of-God) style narrator tells us, "is the largest single celebration of nationalism in Great Britain in the history of the world," a nightmare version of the already nightmare-like opening ceremonies of the Olympics, or worse yet, the halftime show at the Orange Bowl.

With a giant poster of Shorter in his "new look" behind them, the clergy testify to the righteousness of "one faith, one God, one flag" and then introduce "a new superstar in the evangelical firmament," Jeremy Tate, who leads the crowd in the repetition of a single catchphrase: "We will conform." Shorter makes his entrance and stands before a giant cross. His new back-up band gives him the Nazi salute and then commences with the new toned-down Stephen Shorter sound. In the foreground there is still the hokey flag show performed

by "the new British youth," and, as Shorter begins to sing, cripples in wheelchairs are wheeled up to the stage. Shorter touches their heads and they rise to their feet, cured.[25]

The spectacle testifies to the indistinguishability of performance; all performances are essentially the same especially with regard to such a passive audience. The scene ends as the bright color photography of the rally dissolves into a series of black and white still photographs and the narrator concludes: "49,000 people gave themselves to God and flag and Stephen Shorter" (rock culture's newest trinity).

Shorter begins the film—the narrator assures us—as the "most desperately loved entertainer in the world." But unlike the happy-go-lucky Beatles, Shorter is paranoid, nervous, in over his head. He sleeps until noon every day (a familiar symptom of clinical depression), then watches cartoons on television, and, when he bothers to listen to music, he's only interested in his own records. He goes about the daily grind of being a star—interviews, public service appearances, luncheons, concerts—with reluctance and dread.

By the time the National Stadium concert is over, he is on the verge of a nervous breakdown. When he receives an award and a ridiculous statue (a likeness of Shorter, with a revolving phallic-like microphone at waist level that plays his newest hit whenever it is lifted off the table), his acceptance speech is hardly according to the script. "I'm a person," he says, "I'm nothing. I hate you." (Shorter's confession is match-cut with a scene in the Merchants Bank, where the head of Stephen Shorter Enterprises assures us that he was able to get his investors' money out in time.)

The final sequence in the film replays the opening motorcade and ticket tape parade sequence, this time strangely silent. "All that remains of Stephen Shorter," the narrator tells us, "is a couple of old records and this archival footage with the sound, of course, removed." That history can be and is systematically altered offers an obvious allusion to Orwell's *1984*. Such a reference to Britain's most telling and paranoid post-World War II vision seems hardly incidental here. In both *Privilege* and *1984*, big business, with (or as) the government, are shown to be unapologetic and unsubtle in their manipulation. The masses—which both texts depict as passive and stupid—are shown ready and willing to take whatever business and government give

them. *Privilege* ends with a final allusion to *1984*. "It's going to be a happy year," the narrator blankly concludes, "in Great Britain in the near future."

Wild in the Streets (Barry Shear, 1968), an American B-film released the following year, offers an alternative narrative regarding the relationship between rock and roll and fascism, between stardom and a kind of cultural totalitarianism. The film opens as Max, then just a boy, takes LSD, rips the plastic slipcovers off his parents' furniture, and sets fire to the family Chrysler. The rest, we are told by the voice-over narrator, is history, as Max grows from this little rebellious act to be the first rock star/teen idol to become President of the United States.

While Shorter is presented as the overmatched pawn in the complex machinations of corporate and cultural authority and power, Max is depicted as a savvy teen millionaire with ready access to the media and the hearts and minds of America's young. "We're 52% (of the population)," he sings to his under-21 audience, "We make big business big/The economy depends on 52%/You and me." In another song, "14 or Fight," Max demands a vote for every citizen over age fourteen. "We got the numbers now," he intones, "We want the vote now." Ominously, the song concludes with the explicit message: "Kill for the vote."

As his power grows, Max predictably becomes corrupted. "You give me the tools," he announces in a televised address to America's youth, "You give me the power!" Such an obvious call to follow is presented as the logical extension of his influence as a rock star. What makes Max unique is that he decides to exploit this influence in the most conventional way, living out the American dream of wealth and influence and power all the way to the White House.

Once inaugurated, Max incarcerates everyone over thirty in concentration camps and doses them with LSD. After all, Max says early on in the film, "Thirty is death, man." But as the film draws to a close, he himself is approaching premature "middle age." Morose at such a twist of fate, Max finds himself the brunt of the film's final joke. The final scene in the film depicts Max bullying a little boy who is sitting on a dock playing with a crayfish. After he exits the scene, the boy looks directly into the camera and says: "We're gonna put everyone over ten out of business."

Consuming Stardom

In the 1970s rock became more and more a part of the official culture and pop stardom took on the tragic dimensions foreshadowed in *Privilege*. To a great extent, the rock and roll firmament began to resemble Hollywood's. In Don DeLillo's 1973 novel *Great Jones Street,* for example, the fall of fictive rock legend Bucky Wunderlick is foregrounded and foreshadowed by the following breathtaking treatise on fame:

> Fame requires every kind of excess. I mean true fame, a devouring neon, not the somber renown of chinless kings. I mean long journeys across grey space. I mean danger, the edge of every void, the circumstance of man importing an erotic terror to the dreams of a republic. Understand the man who must inhabit these extreme regions, monstrous and vulval, damp with memories of violation. Even if half-mad he is absorbed into the public's total madness; even if fully rational, a bureaucrat in hell, a secret genius of survival, he is sure to be destroyed by the public's contempt for survivors. Fame, this special kind, feeds itself on outrage, on what the counselors of lesser men would consider bad publicity—hysteria in limousines, knife fights in the audience, bizarre litigation, treachery, pandemonium and drugs. Perhaps the only natural law attaching to true fame is that the famous man is compelled, eventually, to commit suicide.[26]

In the novel, Wunderlick's fall is accompanied by significant musical transformations. His plans to produce music that would prompt his audience to "be frozen in pain or writhe with pain [so that] some of them would actually die,"[27] is at once testimony to yet another rock star taking his art a bit too seriously and an apt social commentary on just how loyal loyal fans can be. Wunderlick's understanding of his audience—the Beatles seem oblivious to theirs, Shorter is first intimidated and then discarded by his—is predicated on an understanding of just how profound youth's search for authority really is. "America is out there," DeLillo concludes, "and it's full of people who are waiting to be told what to do . . . America. The whole big thing. Pop music and killer drugs."[28]

While *Great Jones Street* sardonically reveals the passive rock audience, it attends to a very contemporary American mythos: rags to riches to rags. Beset by lunatic fans and the equally lunatic coterie of executives and errand-boys from Transparanoia (the multinational company that controls the management team that controls him) we find Wunderlick living alone, in exile, in hiding, humbled into confessing that "there is so much to be afraid of in contemporary society."[29] The Happy Valley Commune, the hapless but brutal terrorists who dose Wunderlick with an experimental American military drug that blocks his ability to form coherent sounds, to connect with language, do so, we learn, because they are his truest fans. "We are your group image," the terrorists tell him, "We were willing victims of your sound. Now we're acolytes of your silence."[30] But despite it all—and this is DeLillo's ironic message—Wunderlick is still plenty big, rumored to have committed suicide, but like Elvis, rumored to have been seen in various unlikely places here on earth.

The perils of fame is the central theme of *Zazie* (Go Riju, 1989) a Japanese teen film that (however inadvertently) alludes to *Great Jones Street*. Zazie, whose band "Junk" performed songs with lyrics like "I'm just a crazy rebel/My girl calls me a dud/I'm delinquent dynamite/I can't help it if I'm no good/Just dynamite out of control," quits performing at the start of the film. Like Wunderlick, Zazie opts for silence in order to search for meaning and escape his undue influence as a star. But like Wunderlick, Zazie cannot escape his fans. When he finally plans a comeback, he is stopped dead by a former fan who puts a knife in his gut and says: "Why couldn't you just stay a legend?"

A far different view of stardom emerges in the 1980s. In *Purple Rain* (Albert Magnoli, 1984), for example, the iconography, the narrative of stardom, harkens back to the 1930s as Prince (as himself, aka "the Kid") is cast as the talented but as yet undiscovered chorus-line performer awaiting and then seizing his date with destiny.

The ad campaign for the film promises a familiar mythology: "Before he wrote the songs he lived them," and the film follows through. We first see "the Kid" in the Minneapolis nightclub where Prince got his start, performing Prince's songs, filmically rendered in the MTV performance format video style. The point of the film is Prince's

success, a kind of indisputable fact at the far end of an otherwise familiar and at times unpleasant story.

At the heart of Prince's success is his apparent uniqueness, his inaccessibility, his charisma, his difference. His penchant for outrageous and exhibitionist self-expression separates him from his fans, the club manager, his parents, even his fellow performers (including the brilliant Morris Day and the Time and the patently ridiculous Appolonia). Unlike other "professionals," "the Kid"/Prince has little interest in the day-to-day business of making music. He repeatedly misses meetings and is always late for rehearsal. Backstage he is sullen and stubborn. He refuses even to listen to a song Wendy and Lisa, his female band members, tape for his approval. When the women urge him at least to give them a chance, he is abusive and sadistic, first ignoring them, then throwing his voice in falsetto through a monkey puppet on his dressing table. "Next thing you know," the puppet remarks, "they'll want to borrow your motorcycle," insinuating that they are after his power, his machine.

But once the women exit, the puppet cries. The Kid turns on the tape recorder and listens carefully to the song. For those who know Prince's material at all—and who in the audience doesn't?—these first few bars are immediately recognizable as "Purple Rain," the title song of both the film and the album.

In performance—live, on film, and on MTV—Prince takes the risk that he may someday go too far as we see him clutching, humping, masturbating on the floor, dressed like Valentino, Zorro, or Mozart. His range of self-expression testifies to and results from his charisma, his unique masculinity, his elite status.

When in the end the Kid achieves his rightful place in society (as a star) and finally performs his female band members' song, the rest of the cast celebrates his success without reservation. That he toys with sexual difference and vents his rage onstage and off—he ridicules Appolonia when she enters the club with Morris Day and he beats her up after she gives him his signature guitar because she tells him she wants to be a star too—is just part of the package. When he sings "I'm no messiah and you're the reason why," he is never more wrong nor more dishonest. His behavior offstage is irrelevant given the unquestionable and unquestioned conclusion that he is a star. As a result, nothing undercuts the film's adolescent male fable of success.

Purple Rain is both a vanguard movie musical (the first to exploit so systematically the techniques and narrative structures of music video) and a sociological parable (about an undependable young black man perpetuating the cycle of domestic violence, who, unlike Bigger Thomas in Richard Wright's *Native Son,* is fated for something special anyway). Indeed, in Prince's case, though this is hardly an ideal model (but it is one myth of stardom), being a star means never having to say you're sorry.[31]

Along with Prince, Madonna embraces the privileges of the eighties' media-made star. Indeed, she is all image in an age and on a network where image is everything. But unlike Prince, who perpetuates the misogyny that lay at the heart of so much rock and roll, Madonna steals a page from the little-seen teen-movie *Ladies and Gentlemen: The Fabulous Stains* (Lou Adler, 1981) (in which a working-class girl wears her underwear outside her clothing and demystifies the very erotic image she otherwise so depends on) and calls on an egalitarianism and community among the women she is both one of and the ideal for.

"Madonna may be said to represent a postmodern feminist stance," writes E. Ann Kaplan, "combining seductiveness with a gutsy kind of independence." Her success in "articulating a desire to be desired,"[32] Kaplan argues, offers a unique female role model that is at once sexy and plenty interested in sex, a victory for women in the often expensive struggle for fun.

Madonna's penchant for role-playing is essential to her calculated media-male stardom. Indeed, for millions of teenage (and otherwise young at heart) Madonna "wanna-be's," Madonna's make-overs, are somehow empowering. "Madonna worship," argues Nell Bernstein, "is an excuse to put on lipstick and black lace bras, giggle over magazines and shock and impress the guys." But on the other hand, Bernstein quips, such Madonna worship is also "the 1990's version of the consciousness raising group . . . analyzing and emulating *their* pop idol is a means of exploring questions about sexuality, femininity and identity that some feel mainstream feminism rejects."[33]

Madonna "herself," though, is another story. The Madonna Madonna wants you to know and love is brazen and sexy onstage, but hopelessly conservative and Catholic at home. "I deeply respect Ca-

tholicism," she notes in an interview in *Vogue* Magazine, "its mystery and fear and oppressiveness, its passion and its discipline and its obsession with guilt."[34] Such a complex, even contradictory view of Catholicism came under scrutiny after the release of her video for "Like a Prayer," which depicted, among other things, a statue of a sexy black man/religious icon come to life falsely accused of rape and then saved by Madonna's testimony. The interracial romance, her writhing on the altar (à la "Like a Virgin") and the stigmata carved into her hands certainly irked the religious Right, but here again Madonna's supposed risk-taking was much ado about nothing. It may have cost her a Pepsi commercial, but it also affirmed that (only) stars can exhibit such a wide range of behavior. In the sexually uptight eighties and nineties only the stars seem to be having much fun.

MTV, Consumerism, and the New Citizen's Education

"It is the star," writes Lawrence Grossberg, reducing things to the obvious, "who is the major product promoted by music television."[35] The videos that sell these stars—shades of Stephen Shorter here again—are not merely promotions for records or performance tours, but advertisements for consumption as an end in itself. According to Grossberg, "one is always buying more than music when buying rock and roll."[36] Indeed, one is buying a lifestyle, a (hip) attitude, a belief in a hierarchical elitism, and one's own separation from power and transcendence in contemporary society.

MTV is predicated on the assumption of teen anomie; it assumes boredom and lack of motivation or real pleasure. With its rigid and limited playlists, its hip artificiality and its video superstars, it offers a search for happiness in a world where (and the audience knows this) happiness is a ridiculous concept.

MTV is primarily an advertizing network. It insists, for those who are young or just young at heart, on consumption as a kind of psychotherapy. But like all advertisements, it insists, in Stuart Ewen's words, on "projecting commodities as emotional nourishments."[37] For those teens so bored that they are watching MTV—and the station affirms the comic glory of the teen couch potato—the endless barrage

of vertically integrated ads for records, movies, clothing, soft and hard drinks—for listening to music, for going to movies, for buying clothing, for drinking drinks, for watching (M)TV—fill time, youth's most troubling commodity.

"Looking at the world according to advertising," writes Ewen—and how many who cry "I want my MTV" do?—"then looking at our own lives, the fissure between appearance and reality is so great that perpetual disorientation may be its only significant product."[38] The effect of such a disorientation may well be desirable, as it renders irrelevant the significant gap between identity and aspiration, between who we are and what we are willing to believe we can be.

The media, fifties' cultural historian C. Wright Mills argues in convincing counterpoint to Hebdige, Hall, and Frith, forge just such a gap. "The media," Mills writes, "give [us] identity; they tell [us] what [we] want to be—they give [us] aspirations; they tell [us] how to get that way, they give [us] technique; and they tell [us] how to feel that [we are] that way even when [we are] not."[39]

According to a 1990 study, 20 million mostly 11–24 year olds watch MTV every week.[40] The networks' success in assembling a national network of and for youth has prompted a second wave of moral panic over rock music reminiscent of the 1950s. The often violent and prurient and puerile and suggestive images and lyrics in the music videos have helped foreground the networks' dubious "counter-culture" moniker. Such a claim seems wholly unwarranted, except inasmuch as, as Dennis Hopper argued in a recent interview on National Public Radio, "the counter-culture has become the culture."

Accompanying the siege from the Right, traditionally more progressive-minded media critics have also attacked MTV. The Leftist tack cites MTV as yet another lunatic manifestation of contemporary youth-crazed society. Michael Hirschorn, for example, writes: "MTV was—and to some extent remains—a narcotic microcosm of a whole vapid, hype and gratification obsessed era, television raised to the status of cultural condition."[41]

But others on the progressive side have welcomed the music network with open arms. Armed with the "anything goes" of the postmodern condition, E. Ann Kaplan for example, argues that MTV is (at least occasionally) progressive. Her argument hinges on the as-

sumption that MTV is either non-narrative or anti-narrative. Given a second assumption, that all narrative is retrogressive (ie. patriarchal, Oedipal, etc.), the departure from such a tradition is, in and of itself, a step in the right direction. While MTV provides "a 24 hour rapid flow of short segments (that) function as ads"—and here Kaplan embraces precisely what Mills and Ewen lament—if we wade through the morass, we can find subversive forms and thus progressive strategies.[42]

Quite a different argument can be posed if you consider the rapid flow of short segments as pieces in, rather than fragmentations of, a larger narrative: the narrative of MTV. Over a randomly selected two-hour period taped in May, 1990, I found seventy-one distinct segments. Each taken individually indicates a wide variety in subject, style, genre, and even production values. But taken together these segments consolidate a narrative of hip buying patterns: the MTV lifestyle.

Of the seventy-one segments, twenty were national ads and another ten were local spots. Three of the local commercials advertised an insurance company specializing in high risk cases; virtually all of the rest were for food or career-training "colleges." The national commercials fell primarily into six categories: travel, fitness, soft drinks, clothing, cosmetics, and video games. Only thirteen of the seventy-one segments were "actual" music videos, and the play-list included the usual cast of characters: Madonna, Tom Petty, Michael Jackson, Aerosmith, Don Henley, and Guns and Roses. There were eight trailer ads for new movies (all with the teen audience in mind), one short film "from the MTV collection" (an arty little piece by Spike Lee), and four MTV contests, three of which offered the opportunity to "party" with one or another wild MTV-style star. The fourth, the "Vogue-it-up" contest, offered air-time to the ten best lip-synched home videos set to Madonna's hit song "Vogue," which, of course, had been played just minutes earlier.

Most interesting of all, though, were the public service announcements and the three feature stories on the MTV News. Over the two hours randomly selected here, there were five public service spots: two anti-drinking (and driving), two anti-drug abuse, and one pro-environment. The MTV News spots focused on two benefit concerts—

one for the environment, the second calling attention to ex-Eagles drummer Dallas Taylor's search for a liver donor. Taylor himself appeared at the end of the spot, looking emaciated, providing the segment's payoff: "I'm paying the price for a deadly misconception about what it takes to be a rock and roller." In case the moral is still unclear, we cut to the cover of an old Blind Faith album and are told in voice-over that former Blind Faith member Rick Gretsch died of a similar ailment.

The third story focused on Ryan White, the much celebrated, young, white (pre-sexual) AIDS victim who had just died in an Indiana hospital soon after caring visits from (and such is the scope of MTV) Michael Jackson, Donald Trump, John Cougar Mellancamp, and Elton John. An interview with a teary-eyed Mellancamp revealed that while George Bush was "in town," he "didn't bother" to stop by. The newscaster added that Elton John picked up White's hospital tab and dedicated his re-release of a live version of "Candles in the Wind" (about another tragic figure, Marilyn Monroe) to White.

While the videos themselves are alternatingly sexist, racist, and horribly violent, or at best narcissistic and elitist, the overriding message, the "narrative of MTV" is one of good citizenship, conformity, and fitness—feeling, looking, and maybe even doing good. Kaplan's optimism with regard to the anti-narrative segments seems misplaced, as it is these specific fragments that are repressive and retrogressive. But taken as a narrative—taken as a whole—MTV encourages teenagers to care about the environment, to not drink and drive or take drugs, to care about AIDS victims and the starving in Africa. And that is the saving grace of MTV.

The Global Teenager

There are 1.37 billion teenagers in the world.[43] Most of them, contrary to popular belief, are not in the United States. But, it may be argued, they may as well be. The notion of a "global teenager" who is, at base, awfully American, is the subject of a recent study by Will Baker for the *Whole Earth Review*. Surveying 12–20 year olds on every continent—from a variety of cultural conditions and backgrounds—Baker found youth by and large politically conservative and socially

unconscious, tied to their families and schools and communities with a fervor he had not anticipated. What seemed most American about these youths to Baker were their "superficial performances of leisure." Youth "cares about buying things," Baker concludes, "lots of things to wear and drink and drive and listen to . . . they desire a lifestyle, rather than a life."[44]

For Baker, the commodification of youth is a multicultural affair, one whose construct is, at heart, ultimately American. This conclusion is certainly borne out in a recent Pepsi commercial. Here we find the American soft drink and the generation named for it celebrated on the streets of San Francisco by a chorus of 300, 80% of whom are non-white. The jingle's lyrics offer an indicative—and I think chilling—conclusion to this examination of the politics of consumption and youth culture:

> Hello tomorrow
> Your children are here
> Can you hear the new drummer
> The future is clear
> We're taking our place now
> We're grabbing hold
> On a rainbow of promise
> We are your gold
> A generation of change
> A generation of song
> A generation of laughter
> Coming on strong
>
> A generation of color
> Black, white, yellow, red
> A generation of Pepsi
> A generation ahead
>
> We speak the same language
> We share the same voice
> We feel the same feelings
> But we make our own choice
>
> A generation of life
> Now let it be said

ROMANCE AND RUIN

A generation of Pepsi
A generation ahead

Generation
Pepsi generation
A generation ahead[45]

Chapter 5

The Apolitics of Style

The other day I overheard two elderly ladies, cringing as a gang of alarming looking punks passed them, say in tones of horror: "Just imagine what their children will be like." I'm sure a lot of people have said exactly the same about the Teddy Boys . . . and Mods and Rockers. That made me wonder what had happened to them after the phase passed. I reckon they put away their drape suits or scooters and settled down to respectable quiet lives, bringing up the kids and desperately hoping they won't get involved in any of those terrible punk goings on.[1]

As a music lover [Theodor Adorno] hated jazz, likely retched when he first heard Elvis Presley, and no doubt would have understood the Sex Pistols as a return to Kristallnacht if he hadn't been lucky enough to die in 1969.[2]

There Are No Truths, Only Versions[3]

With approximately a generation of youth culture behind it, the punk "movement" in Great Britain was at once spectacular and parodic, and the punks themselves, self-abusive and keenly narcissistic. As punk emerged in the unseasonably hot British Summer of 1976, there could be no doubt; things had hit crisis-time.

From the start, punk was "an unstable mix."[4] Its roots lay in the scrapheap of youth culture(s) gone by: the gender confusion, narcissism, and nihilism of Glam Rock; the paradoxical politique and aesthetics of ugliness of New York punk; and the ritualized dance, drug use, and working-class consciousness of the Northern Soul Movement. Though rooted in white working-class culture and values, the

punks further complicated the mix by idealizing and aping the outlaw mystique of the immigrant West Indian community.

According to Dick Hebdige, the punk appropriation of a marginalized, black community was pure (and simple) provocation. The West Indians were hated because they looked different and because their very presence on the streets served as a reminder of just how dramatically Britain had fallen. Ultimately, the punks simply wanted a piece of the action.

For Hebdige, the punks were "a white translation of black ethnicity"[5]—a point reinforced by punk's celebration of "difference" and by punk music's appropriation of the West Indian reggae sound. But any singular notion of punk—not just such a progressive one— simply does not convince. Indeed, what Hebdige fails to point out is that while the punks embraced aspects of the black community that appealed to them, they also traveled in far more retrograde circles, displaying a penchant for the iconography and ideology of the emerging British Right.

For example, with regard to punk's appropriation of Nazi paraphernalia, Hebdige disconnects the symbols from their racist/fascist roots. For Hebdige, the punks wore Nazi regalia solely to shock. But, then, how are we expected to take signification seriously—which after all is the core of his argument—if certain things mean nothing and others mean a lot, depending on the source and the political implications?

Though well aware of punk's political ambivalence, Hebdige simply can't resist arguing that punk was somehow, despite itself, progressive. He does so with the following cryptic proviso: "(punk) rhetoric is not self-explanatory: it may say what it means but it does not necessarily 'mean' what it 'says.' "[6]

The punks themselves were working class but elitist, anti-fashion but at the same time keenly fashionable. The bricolage Hebdige posits as the heart of punk reveals hopeless contradiction, shock, and provocation as ends in and of themselves. Hebdige sees punk as something truly revolutionary. But in the end, he is mistaking the visceral for the political—the dramatic for the meaningful.

In Hebdige's defense, we can cite the historical and political specificity of punk. Its emergence at a specific juncture in British cultural

history likely was not coincidence or accident. During the fateful, hot summer of 1976, Britain was steeped in the vocabularies of austerity and crisis. Indeed, every day the tabloids were dominated by sensational stories attending to unemployment (especially with regard to youth), unrestricted immigration, and a rising current of violence in the streets (e.g. the neo-fascist/anti-fascist clash in Lewisham and the even more frightening riot at the Notting Hill Street Festival as immigrant blacks fought it out with atypically well-armed police).

Given its emergence in such tumultuous times, punk seems essentially a crossroads youth culture: a moment of truth between sixties' hippie utopianism and the trenchant conservatism of Thatcher's Britain. For Hebdige, and more recently Greil Marcus, the punks were significant because the moment they seized was so crucial.

Rebellion, Refusal, Retrenchment

In *Lipstick Traces: A Secret History of the Twentieth Century*, Greil Marcus opens his teleology of the West with punk's last stand: the Sex Pistols' final concert at the Winterland Ballroom in San Francisco in January, 1978. The concert was, Marcus quips: "as close to the Judgement Day as a stage performance can be."[7] The apocalyptic trajectory of punk is at the core of Marcus's critique. Evidence his description of the band's notorious lead singer, Johnny Rotten: "[Rotten's] aim was to take all the rage, intelligence and strength in his being and then fling them out at the world: to make the world notice; to make the world doubt its most cherished and unexamined beliefs; to make the world pay for its crimes in the coin of nightmare and then to end the world—symbolically, if no other way was open."[8]

But as the glory days of punk came to a close, Rotten, as Andrew Herman puts it, was "sentenced to spend the rest of [his life] in futility trying to recapture the halcyon moment when everything seemed possible."[9] Or, as Marcus describes it, "[Rotten was] condemned to roll [his] greatest hit up the hill of the crowd for all eternity; carrying the curse of having been in the right place at the right time, a blessing that comes to no one more than once."[10] (It is at least ironic that for Marcus the essential romance of punk is revealed in a metaphor to the existential futility of Sisyphus.)

For Hebdige, whose *Subculture: The Meaning of Style* was written while punk remained vital and provocative, the attraction of punk was its perverse glamor, its exoticism, its progressive potential. But for Marcus, who writes well after the fact, critical interest relates a nostalgia for even more earnest and extreme days gone by, when everything, even (or especially) contradiction seemed somehow politically significant.

But both Hebdige and Marcus fall into the same trap. By focusing on stars (Marcus) or an ideal (Hebdige), both ignore the essential apolitics of the punks themselves. Though all too willing to parade their difference, their "other-ness," the punks' refusal to mediate between their own experience and the traditions of their working-class parents—a key project in Hebdige's model—prompted a celebration of dysfunction, a revel in the revelation of "no future." At a moment of truth in the history of British (youth) culture, the punks insisted that nothing before them meant anything and that the future was a nonsensical concept.

Unlike the British skinheads, who attempted, as John Clarke points out,[11] to magically recover (a version of) Britain's "glorious" working-class past, the punks attempted to remove themselves from any such historical project. If, as Hebdige and Marcus argue, the punks deliberately and ritually refused to be a part of the official culture, they did so all the while insisting that their actions were motivated by boredom, by the desire for something, anything to do.

At the core of the progressive argument regarding the progressive politics of punk is a categorical avoidance of the issue of intentionality, of self-consciousness on the part of the punks themselves. Any indulgence of this question leads to another paradox—that the apolitics of punk is somehow romantic (which is hardly progressive). Indeed, when Hebdige attempts to sentimentalize punk, he again makes claims he cannot support: "Punk (seemed) to be parodying the alienation and emptiness which have caused sociologists so much concern, celebrating in mock heroic terms, the death of community and the collapse of traditional forms of meaning."[12] Such a meta-critical edge to punk seems patently absurd. (What sociologists were they reading? From what critical distance was their elaborate parody based?)

Only the bands support Hebdige's idealized punk politique: *viz.* the Sex Pistols' "God Save the Queen" (with the refrain "No future/No future/No future for you") and The Clash's "London's Burning" ("with boredom now"). The punks themselves, Hebdige's great unwashed, hardly support such a heady sociology.

In the final analysis, Hebdige's academic arsenal—Roland Barthes, Henri Lefebvre, Claude Lévi-Strauss, Raymond Williams, and Stuart Hall—overwhelm the book's content. But should all this sound wholly unsympathetic to Hebdige (whose work I rather admire), we need to note that Hebdige elaborates (from a radically new perspective) a methodology for the study of youth that is at once serious and not alarmist, a rare combination indeed. But the punks may well not be Hebdige's best example. (The mods, for example, far better support his claims regarding "the meaning of style.")

Though widely viewed as the seminal work on contemporary youth culture—especially, and deservedly, as the principal methodological tract—Hebdige's *Subculture: The Meaning of Style* has prompted additional reservations, revisions, and critique. In "Defending Ski-Jumpers: A Critique of Theories of Youth Subcultures," for example, Gary Clarke elaborates the essential elitism of Hebdige's project. "The punk creations that are discussed in [*Subculture: The Meaning of Style*]," Clarke asserts, "were developed among the art-school avant garde, rather than emanating from the dance halls and housing estates."[13]

Angela McRobbie provides a second useful qualification of Hebdige. McRobbie points out that Hebdige's emphasis on style as collective experience and his investigation into its "social meaning," renders little of critical use to women and does much to reinscribe the avowedly progressive impetus of style in purely patriarchal terms. Though Hebdige argues for youth's role in challenging cultural hegemony, he does so, McRobbie concludes, by virtually ignoring the role of young women.[14]

Marcus too fails to acknowledge the role of young women in his cultural history. As Andrew Herman notes in a particularly cutting turn of a phrase: "Aside from providing the seductive nostalgic markings to which the title of the book refers, women largely remain a secret in Marcus's secret history."[15] For both Marcus and Hebdige, history is at once sentimental and romantic and rather completely the province of boys and men.

Cash From Chaos

The progressive argument attending to punk by necessity de-emphasizes the role of the subculture's singlemost significant and most problematic figure, Malcom McLaren, the ex-haberdasher gone band manager, the "P.T. Barnum of youth subculture."[16] In *The Great Rock and Role Swindle* (1980), Julien Temple's documentary on the Sex Pistols, McLaren's ability to manipulate the machinery of consumer teen culture at once underscores and undermines the arch political satire of the band's brilliant album, "Never Mind the Bollocks: Here's the Sex Pistols," and their often inspired stage performances.

But despite the triumph of management in an avowedly proletarian subculture, Temple can't help but be seduced by McLaren. We're thirty minutes into the film before the first Sex Pistol has a line of dialogue. When Johnny Rotten finally says "By the time you're 29, you've got two kids and you want to commit suicide," McLaren has already narrated virtually the entire first third of the movie.

"My name is Malcom McLaren," we hear in voice-over over the elaborate opening credit sequence, "and I've done some things in my time. One of the best was punk rock." McLaren's "creative cache" is unquestioned in the film, as he sets down "how to manufacture a group": (1) "minimize the possibility of the press ever actually seeing the group," (2) "find yourself a lawyer who knows nothing about music—he's your best asset," (3) "be as obstructive as possible so that the record company thinks they are getting what they deserve—the bargain of the century," (4) tyrannize and insult your own generation," and (5) "cultivate hatred—create confusion."

McLaren's peculiar entrepreneurship—his ability to be at once charming and smarmy—enabled him to be in cynch with the anti commercial priorities of the subculture and at the same time to be its primary financial benefactor. On the one hand, he played the part of the heartless and greedy manager. On the other, he played the satirist, offering a deft critique of a culture that wholly subscribed to the Weberian capitalist ideal. That either or both may well have described McLaren was epitomized in his credo: "cash from chaos."

McLaren's role in the formation of the Sex Pistols foregrounds his role in their demise. As the engineer of their fame, he became the

overseer of their failure. Indeed, in *The Great Rock and Roll Swindle*, *D.O.A.* (Lech Kowalski, 1981), and *Sid and Nancy* (Alex Cox, 1986)— three films attending to the British punks—the Sex Pistols' story pivots on a single scene set at the Winterland Ballroom in San Francisco. There, in the band's final performance together, we see things on stage going very badly. The camera zooms in (in all three films) on Johnny at center stage venting his disgust: "Ever get the feeling you're being cheated?" In *Sid and Nancy*, the one fictional film, director Alex Cox match-cuts Johnny's speech with a shot of McLaren, glaring down at him from the wings. In the logic of the shot/reverse shot, it is clear that Johnny's remark is meant for him. In the two documentaries, it is unclear exactly what Johnny means or who he is talking to (the audience, the band, himself, McLaren). What is clear in all three films is that this scene marks the end of the road for the band, punk, and its management team.

After the break-up of the Sex Pistols, McLaren—who began his career selling rubber skirts and dog collars at "Sex" (his Kings Road boutique)—managed another band, Bow Wow Wow. For the cover of their first album, he had the band's 14-year-old lead singer pose nude. A close look at the graphic design, though, reveals its allusion to Manet's "Déjeuner sur l'herbe"—McLaren's deft mix and match of cultural taboo (child pornography) and high art. In 1984, McLaren pushed this quintessential punk bricolage one step further, trying his own luck on record sampling dance-beat disco with grand opera.

Four years later, McLaren resurfaced as the subject of a one-person show at the New Museum of Contemporary Art in New York City. McLaren, like punk, had become the stuff of nostalgia. Paul Taylor, the exhibit's curator, aptly titled the show: "Impresario: Malcom McLaren and the British New Wave" and featured "authentic" press clippings and rock videos, artifacts largely collected by McLaren himself.

While promotional material touted the show's postmodern mélange of avant-garde and advertising "art," Taylor remained aware of the exhibition's bottom line. "Hype is the glue of the show," Taylor confessed, "and the sum of its parts. I wanted a show that would get a lot of publicity."[17] And despite excoriating press reviews from the city's high art establishment, "Impresario" delivered as promised, garnering big crowds (just the ticket for a new struggling gallery).

In a review of the show titled, "The Connoisseurship of Hype," Edward Ball concludes that the exhibit had the effect of "turning the museum into a vast reliquary of dead youth culture,"[18] a point of contention unsurprisingly shared by the impresario himself. "The Sex Pistols were my effort to live a waking dream," McLaren reminisced, "The dream lasted about two years. When it was over, all that remained was to collect every press clip we could find."[19]

Following the exhibit's run, McLaren was featured at a symposium, ominously titled "God Save the Spectacle"[20] at New York's Fashion Institute of Technology. There, McLaren shared the dais with punk-musician Richard Hell (the author of the punk anthem, "The Blank Generation") and punk-appropriator and haute fashion designer Stephen Sprouse. Again the project of historicizing punk was at stake, and again McLaren copped the impresario pose.

This time out, McLaren faced a pair of angry hecklers. "You're a pissing shallow exploiter, McLaren," one shouted, "We know where you stand in the class struggle." "I should have stayed home," added the other, "and watched Soul Train." In self-defense, McLaren deigned to agree: "I'm very bourgeois. I never denied that." But on the subject of punk's political agenda—its role in the ongoing politique of youth culture in Great Britain—McLaren waxed nostalgic: "People used to do outrageous things because they meant something. These days, it's for fame, and fame alone. As someone who has had a taste of fame, I can say that it may not be worth it anymore, except to get a good table in a restaurant."[21]

Love Kills

Of the three films focusing on the British punks, *The Great Rock and Roll Swindle* best captures the movement's paradoxical attractiveness and repulsion, its sense of humor and its sense of danger. Unlike his more recent films—*Absolute Beginners* and *Earth Girls Are Easy*—Temple's punk documentary is, in and of itself, ugly. Midgets, naked very young girls and obese women, the elderly and the infirm are all objects of scorn and ridicule. True to the punk aesthetic it so completely embraces, the film espouses obscenity as provocation, ugliness as a metaphor to an otherwise ugly world.

The film is most disturbing when attending to the band's split. After the break-up, Paul Cook and Steve Jones head down to Brazil and form a punk band with Nazi war criminal Martin Bormann. There, the beat and the lyrics remain basically the same. Only the context is different.

Sid Vicious exits London as well as he and his wife Nancy head to Paris. There, Temple stages (à la Busby Berkeley) Vicious's quintessential punk performance of the Frank Sinatra/Paul Anka standard "My Way." In the audience we see a mock-appreciative crowd of pretentious Parisians. The scene offers ample evidence of Sid's utter talentlessness just as it reveals the French aesthetes' tendency to celebrate the basest examples of popular culture from other countries. (See here also the French affection for Jerry Lewis and more recently Mickey Rourke.)

The film's narrative ends with New York newspaper headlines regarding Nancy's murder and Sid's subsequent heroin overdose. But the closing credits refer back to McLaren, as we see an animated sequence depicting the Sex Pistols as pirates being devoured by sharks.

Originally titled *Love Kills*, *Sid and Nancy* testifies to an even more complex and systematic exploitation of the band and, specifically, Sid Vicious. During his fateful two years of stardom, Sid is depicted as an insecure and gullible child, enamoured with the whole punk scene and seemingly unaware of the ways in which Johnny, Nancy, Malcom, his fans, and finally the drugs take advantage of him.

When Sid and Nancy first meet, Sid smashes his head against a wall to get her attention. At first she rejects his advances. But she takes his money (for dope) anyway. Days later they meet again by chance. But he is too naive to realize that she had had no intention of keeping her part of the bargain (of supplying drugs for him as well). Later on in the film, Nancy finally sleeps with Sid, but only after she is rejected by Johnny.

For Cox, Sid is an ingenious innocent, inadvertently honest and perceptive. When Nancy whines, "I don't think Johnny likes me," he instinctively responds, "He doesn't like anyone. He's a fool." When Nancy's father asks Sid if he "plans to make an honest woman" of his daughter, Sid takes the remark at face value and insists, "She's always been honest with me."

Nancy on the other hand is portrayed as a grotesque American groupie, an addict, and a sycophant. Her role in the break-up of the band recalls Yoko's contribution to the Beatles' split. In one scene she and Sid meet the rest of the band in a luncheonette. There she takes on McLaren and Johnny over Sid's contract and plans for the American tour. Cox's depiction of Nancy's role in Sid's dissipation coupled with Chloe Webb's bizarre, shrill performance render her completely unlovable. It is an odd mythology, I know, but *Sid and Nancy* suggests that Sid would not have been half so vicious if not for falling in love with the wrong kind of girl.

Like McLaren, Johnny is portrayed as self-centered and deadly serious, already planning his next move while Sid is busy having fun. As the one band member who truly gets out alive—he now fronts the progressive-punk band Public Image Limited—his savvy counterpoints Sid's childlike naivete. Aware of what McLaren is doing from the start, Johnny is shown to be complicit in the exploitation of the band.

Narratologically, *Sid and Nancy* turns on Cox's faithful restaging of the "My Way" scene from *The Great Rock and Roll Swindle*. After Paris, Sid hits New York and rents a room at the Chelsea Hotel. It is an odd, odd world, the film aptly reminds us, in which Sid and Nancy join the ranks of Dylan Thomas, Thomas Hardy, and Henry Miller—poetic justice, though, despite the hotel manager's insistence otherwise, that they share Edie Sedgewick's drug-altered habit for setting fire to the place.

On stage in Paris, Sid is clearly at the top of his game, but he is also banking on his own fame, his own legend. In New York, his attempt to re-establish himself as a star, or even as a musician fall flat. His failure to garner a new audience testifies to the speed with which youth cultures dispose of such heroes (so long as they remain alive).

In *Sid and Nancy*, McLaren quips: "Sidney's more than a bass player. He's a fabulous disaster. He's a symbol. He embodies the dementia of a nihilistic generation." Hyperbole aside, the film does well to defend such an argument, but also posits just how quickly one generation of youth moves on, and another, with a whole new set of values and rituals, takes its place. While Sid struggles with the burdens of the past, Nancy whines: "At least you *were* something."

114

But in the end, as Terrence Rafferty notes, "Cox makes us see Sid's end as punk's cruel joke on a dumb kid, and the ironies cut the pathos."[22]

Cox successfully debunks the popular academic discussion of punk. Hebdige, for example, parallels the punks' symbolic disfigurement—the bizarre make-up, the masks and aliases—with André Breton's surrealistic ploys "to escape the principal of reality." Surrealism, along with Dada and Futurism, according to Hebdige, foreground punk's insistence on "shock as style." The political aesthetic of collage—for Hebdige, the cut-up style of punk—hinted at a prevailing disorder, a breakdown or category confusion, a self-conscious attempt to erode chronological and epistemological boundaries.[23]

In addition to the however unintentional allusions to Paris in the 1920s, McLaren himself highlighted the relationship between the punks and the Situationist International in Paris in the late 1960s. McLaren's by now famous slogan "cash from chaos," for example, is a reference to the Situationist ideal of *détournement*, the argument that the very contradictions of the official culture could somehow be used in an otherwise revolutionary way. But though the Situationists likely would have tried to make chaos out of cash as well, it is debatable whether or not McLaren followed through.

In the final analysis, punk was ambivalent and ambiguous, its recourse to the materials and materiality of style at once transgressive and elitist, ideologically correct and self-serving. In his review of *Sid and Nancy*, Maurizio Viano observes: "Those who have seen *D.O.A.* will notice that Sid Vicious used to wear a swastika t-shirt . . . whereas in *Sid and Nancy*, he wears one with a hammer and a sickle."[24] That both emblems suit the politique speaks volumes on the paradoxical nature of punk.

Narcissism and Romantic Image of Negation[25]

Much like British punk, the New York variety was by and large a white, urban youth "movement." But while the British punks celebrated the abandon of chaos and extolled the futility of their working-class status, the New York punk *scene* was steeped in a kind of too-hip anomie.

In other words, the New York scene was far more self-consciously aesthetic, far more glib and comical. And though very much an attack on the growing commercialism and elitism of mainstream rock and roll, the bands which comprised the heart of the "movement" proved less predictable (or monolithic) than the British variety. One of the most important New York punk bands were the Ramones (whose British tour did much to influence British punk). The Ramones hail from Queens and, like the Sex Pistols and the Clash, they play fast and loud, garage-band rock and roll. But to augment their pure punk sound, the Ramones ape Beach Boys' harmonies, (sardonically) sentimentalizing mock-moronic lyrics in such titles as "Teenage Lobotomy," "I Want to Be Sedated," and "(I Don't Want to Be a) Pinhead (No More)."

On the other end of the spectrum we find Patti Smith. Smith presented herself as a serious performance artist, juxtaposing "intellectual" pseudo-beat poetry with simplistic, hard-driving rock and roll. While the Ramones insisted that everything was a joke, Smith (via Rimbaud) saw things in a whole different light.

Two "independent" "art" films, *Smithereens* (1983) and *Liquid Sky* (1983), capture the essence of New York punk on screen. In *Smithereens*, we find a young woman, Wren, (modeled after artist Jenny Holzer) using the whole city as her museum, posting, in her case, xeroxed images of herself as signs of her own immanent stardom. She is narcissistic enough, but she tries too hard. Her dreams of stardom or at least fitting in are never realized.

To director Susan Seidelman's credit, while she seems to "dig" the punk scene, she refuses to glamorize it (except in the peculiar anti-glamor of "divine decadence"). At the end of the film, we find Wren wandering aimlessly, alone on the median on a highway where she is mistaken for a prostitute by a fat businessman. Her punk lover has gone West with her money. The young man who loves her and wants to take her "away from all of this" in his Volkswagen Van exits the scene before Wren realizes she cares for someone else besides herself. Her sister in New Jersey is no longer sympathetic since she too has been abused one too many times. By the end of the film, Wren has burned all her bridges behind her and we feel pity, not empathy, for her plight.

Such a decadence of the spirit and the flesh is revealed in *Liquid Sky*, Soviet emigré Slava Tsukerman's cautionary foray into the trendy, bisexual, drug-crazy party scene in Manhattan in the late 1970s. Like *Smithereens*, the film focuses on a young woman, Margaret, played by Anne Carlisle, then a notorious New York punk-club scene-maker. Her penchant for the outrageous, her transformation of fashion into disguise, captures punk's essential narcissism and exhibitionism. Her androgeny and bisexuality are hip and, somewhat ironically, identify her as the film's moral center. (Given that other characters indulge in necrophilia, sexual blackmail, and rape, Margaret is easily the least reprehensible.)

Margaret, we (and she) discover, is empowered by aliens to kill whomever she has sex with. (It's one of the film's many off-color jokes that, since she gets no enjoyment from these encounters, her partners die and she lives.) Her mock-moronic comment on all of this—"I kill with my cunt"—is underscored by her (and the film's) rather perceptive and progressive view of gender and sexual relations.

For example, at the end of the film, when those around her have gone the way of all flesh, Margaret sits in front of her mirror and paints her face (like a clown). "You want to know where I'm from?," she asks, looking directly into the camera, "I'm from Connecticut. I was taught that my prince would come and he'd be a lawyer. We'd have two kids and we'd have a barbeque. And all the other people would come. And they'd say, 'Delicious, delicious.'' Oh, how boring.'' Such a social comment, however appropriate, is rendered suspect, alien, as the speech extends into punk sarcasm and obscenity: "I was taught that one should be fashionable. And to be fashionable is to be androgenous. And I'm as fashionable as David Bowie. And people say I'm beautiful. And I kill with my cunt. Isn't that fashionable?"

Margaret's speech continues, extending the treatise on gender and sexual politics. Cynically pointing out that being androgenous and bisexual has hardly made her happy—indeed she is raped by both men and women in the film—she commits suicide and boards the alien spaceship in the strange finale of the film.

As Janet Bergstrom points out about *Liquid Sky*, the punk subculture depicted in the film is "characterized by a sense of its own outsider status, to the point of extreme, narcissistic, self-destructiveness; lack

of emotion, other than derisiveness or hostility; attention to surface, as seen in the fashion obsession, the importance of being in costume, the Club; and forms of dependency, especially drug dependency and the passivity associated with it."[26] Punk is, in the end, dominated by ambience, a *withdrawal* into style.

The Para-Punk Underground[27]

The New York punk scene survives today in the very art(y) underground from which it began some fifteen years ago. These days, the punk sensibility—its style, its politique, such as it has ever been—lives on onscreen in the very marginal(ized), often super-8mm cinema and video of Beth and Scott B. (*Black Box* [1978] and *G-Man* [1978]), Charles Ahearn (*The Deadly Art of Survival* [1979]), Vivienne Dick (*Beauty Becomes the Beast* [1979]), Nick Zedd (*Geek Maggot Bingo* [1983] and *They Eat Scum* [1979]), Eric Mitchell (*Kidnapped* [1978] and *Red Italy* [1978]), and Richard Kern (*Manhattan Love Suicides* [1985], and *The Right Side of My Brain* [1985]).

At the heart of these films is a purposefully shocking expression of urban alienation and despair. But given the milieu of divine decadence, there is also the tendency to render sociopathy and pathology hip and aesthetic, enviable and rational. Additionally, these films often seriously examine gender relations, but do so against the retrogressive backdrop of hard-core pornography.

Certainly, as with the British punks, the appropriation of the iconography of pornography is problematic. Kern's *The Right Side of My Brain*, for example, functionally splits the sound and image tracks; while we hear Lydia Lunch recite a proto-feminist diatribe about men, we see her in various masturbatory activities and in explicit scenes of her own sexual exploitation. In the ad copy for Kern's work, one finds the lingo of the XXX crowd, further confusing these films' role *vis à vis* a hip or progressive audience.

Kern's gesture to 42nd Street characterizes a large segment of the post-punk fallout in New York. But another faction of this para-punk underground looks and plays altogether differently. Here I am referring to the work of Eric Mitchell, whose muse seems rather obviously Andy Warhol. In *Kidnapped*, for example, Mitchell glibly re-presents

the affectless drug culture of those halcyon days at the Factory via a blank, seemingly unmediated visual style with long, awkward scenes in which Mitchell himself appears in the film directing his actors and elaborating lighting strategies. Like so many of Warhol's early "shorts," *Kidnapped* ends as Mitchell runs out of film.

Mitchell's elaborate homage to Warhol is hardly inadvertent or unique. The idiotic violence, exhibitionism and narcissism, keen fashion sense, and penchant for irony and bad-taste black comedy that characterizes the New York punks all seem rooted in the peculiar ambience of Warhol's arty sixties counter-culture. Of note here as well are the similarities between Warhol and McLaren, glib impresarios, at once the center of a movement they otherwise feed off of, odd authority figures rather heartlessly profiting nicely off the talents of those around them.

The L. A. Punks: It's Kiss or Kill

Punk surfaced in Los Angeles in the late seventies as a curious blend of anarchy and anomie—self-consciously representing itself as a last desperate attempt for white, urban lower middle-class youths to express their distaste for a society that had long since expressed its disinterest in them. For the duration of its brief hold on the disenfranchised youth of urban Los Angeles (roughly from 1977 to the first few years of the 1980s), punk unapologetically paraded a variety of misanthropic and misogynist tendencies: Nazism, fascism, racism, and self-hate. No American youth movement before or since has laid so bare the desperation residing at the heart of the now-failed urban American dream.

As a rejection of the late seventies/early eighties gearing up of the yuppie lifestyle, the Los Angeles punks paraded a glib and steadfast embrace of the frustrations inherent to their outsider status, maintaining an essential insider subculture—one which was simply too extreme to court the likes of the urban bourgeoisie as anything more than dumbfounded spectators. Punk performance—here a very broad term indeed—generally manifested itself in ritual terms, shared acts or activities displaying a ceremonial and privileged significance. Punk attire and behavior opposed convention, which was consistent with

the movement's tendency towards celebrating its members' alienation from the mainstream of bourgeois city life.

Two films, both by former UCLA film school students who were in
Los Angeles in the late seventies, articulate (for audiences outside
the scene) the essence of the Los Angeles punks: Penelope Spheeris's
documentary, *The Decline of Western Civilization* (1981) and Alex
Cox's *Repo Man* (1984), a fictional film that purposefully juxtaposes
the punk hallmark anti-commercialism to the crude narratives and
visual styles of truly bad B-films.

From the opening credit sequence to the closing scene hovering
above the night-lit city in a radioactive automobile, *Repo Man* leaps
and lunges from one thing to the next, never effacing, in fact celebrating the anti-aesthetics of the low budget B-movie. Much of the
film is comical and ridiculous, banking on postmodern pastiche,
kitsch, and camp. The film features aliens, a radioactive car, and an
obscure plot involving repo men battling g-men. The film's truth-
teller, Miller, who waxes philosophical while burning garbage under
the striking Los Angeles smog sunset, talks about the cosmic rele-
vance of "plates of shrimp" and argues that (in of all places Los
Angeles) "the more you drive the less intelligent you are." His rev-
elations are characteristically off-center, which explains why he has
such authority in the film.

Repo Man rather blankly wades through hackneyed dialogue reminiscent of the strained seriousness of fifties' B-movie teenage melodramas, as evident in the following dialogue: Duke (dying from a
gunshot wound suffered while robbing a convenience store): "I know
a life of crime has led me to this sorry fate. And yet I blame society—
society has made me what I am." Otto (the punk cum repo man hero
of the film): "That's bullshit. You're a white suburban punk just like
me." Duke: "But it still hurts," (and then he dies).

The helter-skelter pace of the film punctuates the searing punk
music score; it compliments the punk ambience. Scenes appear and
disappear without much coherence or authorial organization, as if any
pretense to narrative order would betray the punk sensibility of the
film. But despite its B-movie clichés and scatterbrained narrative,
Repo Man successfully posits a realistic and depressing view of the
city and its youth.

When Kevin, Otto's straight friend, mindlessly stacks and prices cans of generic peaches in a small city supermarket, he sings the 7-Up jingle ("Feelin' 7-Up/I'm feelin' 7-Up"). Later on in the film, Kevin peruses the want ads. "There's room to move as a fry cook," he says, "in two years I'll be assistant manager. It's key!" Otto at first rejects such an acquiescence. But his heroism is soon undercut as he unremorsefully enters the repossession business.

Eugene, the young punk who opens *The Decline of Western Civilization* with a treatise on how punk has "no stars—no bullshit," expresses his rationale for "rebellion" via vague references to buses and poseurs. For him, as for so many other punks, the city is both subject and object, at once sacred and profane. *Repo Man* similarly attends to the significance of the city to Los Angeles' punk culture. The film's focus on the unglamorous, East Los Angeles city-scape as opposed to the fun, sun, and surf allure of Santa Monica, Malibu, or Venice (where the majority of mainstream television shows and cinema are shot) depicts the city as just one large bad neighborhood; indeed, the film's two principal protagonists meet at the far end of a single tracking shot, traversing street litter, an automobile graveyard, and obscure punk graffiti.

Of the many punk rituals depicted in *Repo Man*, perhaps the most dramatic is the phenomenon of pogo. A dance done to music executed at 250 beats per minute (disco, for example, is performed at half that speed), pogo (and its offspring, the even less structured slam) was pure and simple the performance of violence. Whereas (as I see it) mainstream rock and roll sugarcoats an essential misanthropy and misogyny as teenage romance and rebellion, the punks accepted the "teenage wasteland" for what it is. Punk was the celebration of resignation. It was anomie as artistic impulse. And in a cult of aggressive egalitarianism (everyone is worthless/everyone is the same) everyone involved in the punk performance was part of the performance.

In *The Decline of Western Civilization*, and this is to Spheeris's credit (and coincident with her decision to document rather than comment on the scene), the concert material featured in the film is almost exclusively shot from the point of view of the audience. There the camera is obscured, jostled, harassed, threatened, knocked over, kicked and cursed and abused by the maniacal pogo-dancing punks.

In a particularly clever vignette, Spheeris films a training session for security guards slated to work a punk show. "Actually there is no difference between dancing and fighting," the bouncer-instructor tells them as he grabs a security-trainee by the throat. Shaking his new co-worker like a rag doll he sarcastically adds, "This, for example, is dancing."

Despite, or perhaps because of its penchant for ritualized violence, misanthropy, and misogyny, the punk movement in Los Angeles has courted its share of progressive political attention. Fred Pfeil, for example, argues that *Repo Man* "reproduces the relation between the bone-numbing vacuity and circularity of daily life," noting that the film's "sudden jolts of idiotic violence"[28] offer a profound (Pfeil would argue postmodern) critique of "the nowhere city."[29] Pfeil then comments on "the simultaneous desire and dread of some ultimate, externally imposed moment of truth" in *Repo Man*—a moment that "once and for all would put an end to the endless, senseless repetitions of which our lives seem to be made."[30]

But underscoring, at times undermining, the progressive politics of *Repo Man* is its vicious sarcasm—a mode of address that proved seductive to the film's intended, well-educated, white audience. A similar sarcastic edge proliferated the punk fanzines like *Wet*, *Slash*, *the Lowest Common Denominator*, *Contagion*, and *No Mag*. Targeted at the punks themselves, these magazines were characteristically absurdist and existentialist, graphically misanthropic, racist, misogynist, and wryly comic (like *Repo Man*).

For example, a mock advertisement in *Wet* touts a solar power electric chair. The ad is headlined: "Organic Executions for the Sunbelt." The real-looking advertisement credits the chair to New York designer James Hong and guarantees that the device is effective "even on a partly cloudy day." The chair, as advertised, has a "slow rotisserie" mode, with "capabilities for torture most of us haven't dreamed about since the days of the Protestant Reformation." And with a typical bit of (not really tongue-in-cheek) punk social theory, the ad concludes: "Just the thing to stamp out those food stamp cheating single mothers."[31]

Punk and The Politics of Rock and Roll

The self-effacing, self-mutilating, self-abusive tendencies of punk—shared by its performers and fans to the point of establishing the movement's most significant bond—were dramatically performed in ceremonies of complete sexual and physical surrender. Punk slam and pogo dancing guaranteed physical injury. The indiscriminate use of drugs and alcohol among the punks involved none of the glamor and pretense to being cool so often associated with mainstream rock and roll. For punks, substance abuse was not a case of individual out-of-control behavior (like, say, Jimi Hendrix or Janis Joplin), but a chosen, group ritual act of self-destruction—Jonestown set to music. For punks the culture *en masse*, including that of rock and roll, is senseless and stupid; to punks, rock glamor, romance, and petty teen-age *angst* are comical and unacceptable.

This sense of desperation is captured in the music. In *The Decline of Western Civilization*, journalist Brenden Mullen calls punk the folk music of the 1980s, and in the purest sense of the term folk he is right. The songs, the baiting, the heckling, and the fistfights between band members and the crowd establish and maintain a bizarre form of kinship. For punks, the self-destructive rituals constitute a group bond far more uniform and cohesive than Woodstock or Altamont or Live Aid ever provided (an attitude which is not at all dissimilar to that of many British football fans who risk death to cheer on their teams).

Since the advent of Tin Pan Alley, the cultural significance of popular music has been the subject of a rather divergent debate. Some culture critics, here most notably the proponents of the Frankfurt School, focus on the almost immediate commodification of pop music by the culture industry. In "On Popular Music" for example, Theodor Adorno draws a parallel between mass market assembly-line commodity production and the production techniques inherent to the "Tin Pan Alley music industry," two factory operations that effectively standardize their product. "Standardization," writes Adorno, "keeps listeners in line by doing their listening for them."[32] This "pre-di-

gested" music "lulls the listener to inattention. [It] tells him not to worry for he will not miss anything."[33] Such a suspicion of pleasure characterizes Adorno's sense of "a masochistic adjustment to authoritarian collectivism," in which the machine-like beat mimics the very rhythms of industrial exploitation, coalescing, in Adorno's terms, "the personality of the obedient."[34]

Adorno's view of popular culture as primarily escapist and sentimental is part of a larger argument regarding the structuration of power, "the machinery of domination" in contemporary society. Reconciled to "social dependence," the audience of such standardized popular music enjoys a seeming mass catharsis; but, as Adorno warns, [it is] a catharsis that keeps them firmly in line." In a thinly veiled reference to the totalitarian project that seemed to be succeeding in Europe in 1941 when he wrote "On Popular Music," Adorno chillingly concludes: "One who weeps does not resist any more than one who marches . . . When the audience at a sentimental film or sentimental music becomes aware of the overwhelming possibility of happiness, they dare to confess to themselves what the whole order of contemporary life ordinarily forbids them to admit, namely, that they actually have no part in happiness."[35]

In punk, Adorno's fears regarding the repetitive and reductive tendencies of popular music are dramatically played out, but to a significantly different ideological effect. Punk music is fast, loud, and for the most part simplistic. The songs—at least in the Los Angeles variety—seldom last more than a scant two minutes and are often, musically, indistinguishable from one another. Los Angeles punk bands like the Circle Jerks actually highlighted the indistinguishability of their songs. Every Circle Jerks number reveals an identical chord pattern. One song begins as another ends. There are no refrains, no codas, no hooks, and no payoff endings. This standardization, so abhorred by Adorno and so much a part of his critique of the culture industry, is in punk music part of a unifying, egalitarian ritual, one which effaces rather than emphasizes the distance between the performer and the audience.

In *Sound Effects: Youth, Leisure and the Politics of Rock 'n' Roll*, Simon Frith extends this notion of an active, participatory audience to all of rock and roll. "There is no moment," Frith argues, "in which

[rock and roll] records are passively consumed, simply used up." In direct opposition to Adorno's absolutist paranoia, Frith contends that rock and roll records are actively consumed, *used* "in contexts of leisure that are not easily controlled."[36] Indeed, Frith concludes, whatever the culture industry has in mind, the teen consumers redefine and redirect it in the very act of consuming the product.

Frith's overall argument hinges on the relationship between rock and roll and the function(s) of leisure in youth culture. "The truth about youth culture," he posits, "is that the young *displace* to their free time the problems of work and family and future." While leisure rather reinforces the alienation of work for adults by providing a structured and defined "escape," the young, because they "account for their lives in terms of play, focus their politics on leisure."[37] For youth, leisure is not an escape, it is life itself.

Cognizant of the problematic role of moneyed interests in the organization (e.g. the production and distribution) of youth-oriented leisure and rock and roll, Frith challenges the culture industry approach by problematizing the relationship between capital investment and social control, arguing that the meaning of rock and roll somehow transcends its industrial base. But looking at this another way, one could argue that much of rock and roll suggests a capital investment in teen discontent and the engendering of teen discontent for profit. In such an argument—which provides the flip-side of Frith's—in the act of consuming, youth revels in the discrete heroism of anomie and thus remains separated from the political mainstream. Such, in the end, are the consequences of their abandon to consumption.

Frith's point of view is shared by Lawrence Grossberg, who, in his essay, "Is There Rock After Punk?," argues that "the power of [rock and roll] music lies not in what it says but in what it does."[38] Like Frith, Grossberg contends that it is a record's specific audience that "invests" meaning in the music—that music allows teenagers to metaphorically put their mark on *their* music, on a small piece of a world that otherwise incessantly and rather systematically puts its mark on them. As to the problematics of industrial control, Grossberg argues that rock and roll coordinates and defines "the possibilities for both domination and resistance." For Grossberg, and this is about as antithetical to Adorno's argument as one can get, pleasure in and of

itself is a form of empowerment (in rock and roll because of the intrinsic relationship between the music and the pleasures of the body).[39] Ultimately, both Frith and Grossberg refuse to acknowledge the culture industry's exploitation of pleasure as divertissement, as escape, as acquiescence. For them, the consuming power of youth is just too strong.

Bernard Gendron connects such idealism with Hebdige's argument regarding youth's systematic disruption of post-World War II hegemony. Gendron views rock and roll's "appearance at a particular juncture of class, generational and cultural struggle [as] an instrument of opposition and liberation."[40] He paraphrases Hebdige when he writes, "One cannot understand the meaning of a rock and roll record without situating it within the youth cultures which typically consume it. In effect . . . the punks rewrite the recorded text . . . by recontextualizing it within their practices and rituals."[41] Gendron connects such an anti-auteurism with Roland Barthes's concept of a "readerly text," positing the following familiar ideological conclusion: "If either the artist or the consuming public is the primary creator of . . . meaning, then rock and roll does have the liberatory power so often claimed for it."[42]

However we view the function and significance of popular music, the issue of the specific ideological agenda of punk remains a difficult issue. The songs performed by X, Black Flag, the Circle Jerks, the Germs, Catholic Discipline, and Fear that comprise much of *The Decline of Western Civilization*, feature overtly political lyrics, but given the problematics of authorial intention the precise point is rendered obscure or paradoxical. Black Flag, for example, a band fronted by an Hispanic lead singer, performs "White Minority," a fascist, racist rant made altogether paradoxical by the lead singer's ethnicity. Another of their songs, "Depression," heralds a conventional rock and roll sentiment, teenage *angst*, but with an at once ironic, angry, and desperate subtext: "Got no friends/No girls want to touch me/I don't need your fucking sympathy."

X, like Black Flag, matches high speed rhythms essential for pogo and slam dancing with exaggerated, even grotesque rock and roll lyrics. "Nausea," for example, about vomiting blood after drinking too much, is a classic bar song, but with a shifted focus to the morning

after; and "Johnny Hit and Run Pauline," which uncritically tells of a violent rape fantasy, takes the mainstream rock and roll penchant for misogyny and sexual violence to bizarre and graphic extremes. In "We're Desperate," X affirms the apolitics of punk teen anomie: "We're desperate/Get used to it/We're desperate/It's kiss or kill."

In the late seventies, the most interesting bands made their reputations by getting barred from one club or another for inciting riots. Black Flag, for example, introduces one of their numbers in *The Decline of Western Civilization* with the following: "This song is for the L.A.P.D. We got arrested the other night for playing punk rock music. They called it a public nuisance. This song is for them and it's called 'Revenge'."

Since the pretense to musicianship and professionalism had come to characterize mainstream, commercial rock and roll, many of the Los Angeles punk bands made a spectacle out of their own lack of musical talent. To punks, in this celebration of the amateur lay the seeds of a true egalitarian, proletarian art, one supported by standardization and simplicity.

Here the Germs provide a most telling example. Germs' performances were never organized around songs but "gained meaning" from the bizarre ramblings and completely drug-altered behavior of their lead singer Darby Crash. Though the band simply could not play their instruments, and Crash could not sing, each performance was, at least, spontaneous and unique.

As it may not have been evident at the time, Crash's onstage performance was a thinly veiled public suicide ritual. What had its perversely funny moments—Crash's habit of forgetting to sing into the microphone for example—also had its darker side. Every Germs performance ended with Crash hurling himself limp-limbed into the audience. When he'd emerge he'd be effaced with magic marker drawings all over his face and chest, or worse, cut by a knife or a piece of glass in the melee on the floor. When Crash died of a drug overdose at the height of his "fame," he became the movement's unlikely martyr, its rebel, its James Dean.

Though terms like "star" and "fame" were anathema to the punks, Crash was the movement's best-known figure—a scene-maker who precisely because of his lack of true star qualities (charisma, attrac-

tiveness, wit, etc.) became a punk legend. His death, a familiar fate to so many punks who similarly abused drugs, seemed appropriate. Like Dean's death, it symbolized living fast and dying young to his teenage fans.

Of all the bands featured in *The Decline of Western Civilization*, Fear is the most provocative and charismatic. In their set, which closes the film, their lead singer Lee Ving purposefully provokes the audience. In response to a heckler, Ving shouts: "Next time don't bite so hard when I cum." Preceding their final number, Ving attacks the slimy deal-makers from the record companies: "If there are any A&R people out there, go die." Later, when he mocks homosexuals ("We're from Frisco," he says hanging his wrist limply, "We think you're a bunch of queers") or when he says "You know why chicks have their holes so close together? . . . So you can carry them around like sixpacks," his disdain for public propriety is the point of his performance; it is the only real rationale for performance. But whether or not to take Ving at his word is another matter entirely.

Fear's live set includes: "Beef Bologna" (revealing Ving's girl-friend's taste with regard to cuts of meat), "Let's Have a War" ("So you can go die"—Fear's answer to the population explosion), "I Don't Care About You (Fuck You)," and "I Love Livin' in the City" (lyrics as follows: "My house smells just like a zoo/It's chock full of shit and puke/Cockroaches on my walls/Crabs are crawlin' on my balls/Oh, I'm so clean-cut/I just want to fuck some slut/I love livin' in the city . . . Suburban scumbags/They don't care/They just get fat/And dye their hair/I love livin' in the city"). Their performance, which displays punk at its most visceral—at its most attractive and repulsive—closes with a satire on the national anthem: "O'er the land of the free/And the homos and Jews." To conclude the obvious, the argument regarding the progressive politics of punk hardly holds together here.

Chapter 6

The Road to Ruin

"One recurrent aspect of popular culture," writes Dana Polan, "is its self-reflexive dimension—its pointed commentary on, and even pastiche or parody of, its own status as a cultural item."[1] For Polan, the various narratives that comprise popular culture are at once intertextual—i.e. part of a flow of "meaningful units" that bear a multitude of cultural implications—and incoherent ("in the literal sense of the inability or unwillingness of a culture to cohere, to follow evident logic").[2]

These "units" then become part of "a vast spectacle," an intertwining of contemporary social relations.[3] Given such a model, Polan quips: "the new mass culture may operate by offering no models whatsoever, preferring instead a situation in which there are no effective roles that one could follow through from beginning to end."[4]

In the wake of punk, and its insistence on "no future," and given Polan's apt sense of the non-sense of eighties' postmodern popular culture, we need not be surprised by the teen film's recent regression, its shift into what Fredric Jameson terms "la mode rétro," the nostalgia mode.[5] For Jameson, the descent into nostalgia is accompanied by the "emergence of pastiche" (instead of parody). This "neutral practice" of "speaking in dead languages," in Jameson's view, leads to "an imprisonment in the past"[6] and signals a wholesale "failure of the new." But as Jameson aptly concludes: "while we seem condemned to seek the historical past through our own pop images and stereotypes"—such is the futility of the historical project these days— "[the past] itself remains forever out of reach."[7] "In a world in which stylistic innovation is no longer possible," Jameson concludes, "all

that is left is to imitate dead styles."[8] In the absence of culture, there is, at least, nostalgia.

Nostalgia as History

It is at once ironic and appropriate then that recent nostalgia films have been heralded by many critics as stylistically and narratologically innovative, as daring forays into previously unexplored possibilities of commercial cinema. Under the mask of parody and pastiche, the majority of these films wallow in a past that never existed, a past wholly comprised of images and plots from our shared past as spectators, as viewers.

An apt example here is the bittersweet *Edward Scissorhands*, a 1990 Christmas release that at once embraces the chiaroscuro visual style and penchant for the grotesque characteristic of German Expressionism and the sun-lit innocence and idealism, the simplistic morality of the seventies generation's prevailing nostalgic scene, television's *Happy Days*.

Edward Scissorhands takes place in any-suburb, U.S.A. where all the houses are the same design, the cars are American and mid-sized, and the streets are clean and empty. But there is an inherent hideousness to such a banal landscape. The houses are painted in ridiculous candy-colors and clash horribly with each other. When the army of male commuters heads off to work, their cars all at once emerging from behind automatic garage doors, the color scheme goes from bad to worse. The women they leave behind every day at the same time settle down to a routine of housework, gossip, and daytime television; they dress in bed-jackets and stretch pants, sport hair-rollers and garish scarves.

To director Tim Burton's credit, the bucolic suburban vision is at once serene and hideous; the women, self-effacingly comical yet capable of unself-conscious cruelty. For Burton, beneath the serenity and idiocy of the media's middle America lies a heart as black as coal.

Enter Edward, an automaton and a freak, a naive whose only crimes are true love (for Kim, the film's narrator and primary love interest) and a belief in the homespun platitudes of Kim's father regarding *laissez faire* capitalism, fair play, and the American dream. Edward's

embrace of a nostalgic and simplistic rags-to-riches philosophy is at first supported by his meteoric success, for in short order he transforms from freak to entrepreneur.

But the film's blank depiction of Edward's unbelievable acquisition of fame and success, its deft elision of conventional markers of time and place renders such a narrative absurd, anachronistic, ahistorical. What Edward learns—what he discovers from his experiences (his narrative)—is that success is fleeting, empty, and perilous. Indeed, while the film begins as the stuff of *Happy Days*, it ends steeped in the dire pessimism of eighties and nineties downward mobility.

Like David Lynch's *Blue Velvet* (1986), there's a sense that *Edward Scissorhands* is about the underlying savagery of middle America. And as in *Blue Velvet*, tone is at once the key and most baffling element of the narrative. For example, at the end of *Blue Velvet*, Lynch closes off the narrative in the goofiest terms available as we see the romantic couple (who have been exposed to a range of perversities throughout) look out the kitchen window at a wooden robin feeding on a worm. We hear soft, airy music in the background and then we cut to the exotic, masochistic Dorothy who has up to then been brutally handled; she's wearing mundane clothes and her recently kidnapped little boy is smiling, as if he has not just lost his father to murder. Peace has been restored to the small town, but it is, in its way, as strange as the preceding violence.

Burton is less arch, less sarcastic at the end of *Edward Scissorhands* and as a result is less likely to be misunderstood. As quickly and inexplicably as they accept Edward, in a manner that would have suited Frank Capra, the neighborhood turns on him. In the end, he is too "different." They want him out of their neighborhood and they get their way. For Burton, the social comment here seems to be that the past simply cannot persist into the present—perhaps, given its absurd simplicity, it may be that the past never really existed at all. History, rarely a high priority in the teen movie, is in the recent run of nostalgia films in exceedingly short supply.

Burton begs a key question here *vis à vis* the postmodern debate. Is, as Jameson suggests, the nostalgia film the paradigm of postmodernism? Or does narrative time no longer exist in the linear, relative sense? Burton seems to have it both ways, which may well be an apt

Easy Rider (Dennis Hopper, 1969) and *The Graduate* (Mike Nichols, 1967) suggested the end of the genre. In doing so it suggested that the image of youth that worked some twenty years earlier was still the image of youth people preferred to see, perhaps even believed was essentially real and true.

Though its style is overwhelmingly buoyant, *American Graffiti* is narratologically bittersweet. As Lucas himself put it: "I was very aware of the changes taking place around me as I was growing up and I loved it, but at the same time it was sad."[10] With that in mind, Lucas used *American Graffiti* to focus on youth on the cusp of adulthood, teens taking full advantage of one last night of lunatic adolescence before the long ugly haul of adulthood.

The characters in the film are at once attractive and laughable. Their desperation—this is their last night, after all—is a source (for us, no doubt) of exhilaration, nostalgic euphoria, and embarrassment. Though the film was widely viewed—by Paramount Studios, by the advertising and marketing crews, by the vast majority of its audience—as an upbeat film, Lucas's attempt to examine the darker side of his own youth does indeed surface. Robert Hatch, film critic for the *Nation* at the time, described the film as "an intricate, almost solemn pageant." Though seduced by Lucas's visual style and the performances of the (then unknown) ensemble cast (Ron Howard, Richard Dreyfuss, Harrison Ford, Paul LeMat, Cindy Williams, and Candy Clark), Hatch concluded that *American Graffiti* confirmed his suspicions that "this drive-in, milk-shake and french-fries, whaddyaknow? world" (that is adolescence—even in its most idealized form) "is overpoweringly boring."[11]

Citing the film's conformist subtext, Hatch aptly notes that "all the boys and girls are listening to the same crude disc jockey, all eating the same junk food, all seeking status and trying to invent excitement."[12] Indeed, the film chronicles youth endlessly cruising the strip, in search of a thrill but rarely if ever finding it. For example, John, the legendary drag racer, "cruises some chicks," but ends up with somebody's little sister. When Toad cruises (in Steve's car) for the first time ever, he picks up a ditzy blonde, gets drunk, then beat up, loses, then finds the car. In the end, as Laurie goes off with Falfa, Steve takes the car back, humiliating Toad in front of his date. Curt's

night is similarly frustrating. His search for the blonde in the white T-bird ends with his discovery of the impossibility of their ever getting together, of his ever getting what he wants without leaving town.

John's predicament—residing, like the other characters, on the verge of adulthood—is perhaps the most daunting, precisely because he has the furthest to fall. Testimony to Lucas's affection for the antinomies of the movie Western (see also *Star Wars* I, II, and III), John is depicted as an aging gunslinger (at 18!), already nostalgic for the good "old" days. "Used to be you could cruise for hours," he says early on in the film, "it was really something." Later, when he and Carol (the teeny-bopper he "picks up" on the strip) go to a junkyard, John waxes philosophical: "I've been just quick enough to stay out of this graveyard." Though Carol adds, "You've never been beat," John realizes his existential dilemma, i.e. the inevitability of growing old, of losing a step, of someone younger and faster coming along gunning for him. For John, as for no one else in the film, the end of youth is potentially catastrophic.

When John and Falfa, the outsider with a hot car and a cowboy hat, finally do race at the end of the film, the scene is brief and anti-climatic. Falfa leads out of the gate but almost immediately loses control of his car. The scene takes no longer than few seconds—a not particularly dramatic, but realistic duration for such a race. Victorious, John is a good winner because he's resigned to the surety of eventual defeat. "The man had me," he tells Toad, "he was beating me." But Toad insists on the legend. "You don't know what you're talking about," he says, "it was the most beautiful thing I ever saw. You'll always be number one. You're the greatest."

For Toad, the stability and authority of John's heroism is like an anchor in an unsteady sea. Toad is not graduating. He gets one more year of youth and he's frightened to death of what that means. John at first shrugs off Toad's hero worship, but then gives in: "OK Toad, we'll take them all." But his tone is perceptibly maudlin. Even in victory, he epitomizes the quintessence of nostalgic loss; nostalgia, after all, is always about loss. As Steve, the most traditional of the youths affirms early on in the film, "You can't stay 17 forever." Why anyone would want to may well be the ironic moral of *American Graffiti*, a film advertised and largely viewed as a celebration of the glory days of youth.

Testimony to the influence of Coppola and "his" sound engineer Walter Murch, in *American Graffiti* the 1960s pop music package contextualizes the film's otherwise episodic structure. When Curt first sees his dream girl, we hear "Why Do Fools Fall in Love?" When Steve and Laurie go to the hop, we hear "At the Hop," then "She's So Fine," "(Oh) To Be A Teenager in Love," and, after they argue, the bittersweet "Smoke Gets in Your Eyes." When Toad picks up Debbie, we hear "Almost Grown," and later, when he waits outside the liquor store for a passerby to buy booze for them, we hear "Maybe Baby." When Curt is "recruited" by the teen gang, the Pharoahs, we hear "The Great Pretender." Then, the gang forces Curt to sabotage a police car and we hear "Aint That A Shame." When he's successful, we hear (as the car is split in two) "Come and Go With Me." When Curt accompanies the Pharoahs as they rob the local mini-golf we hear "Get a Job." When Laurie gets into Falfa's car on his way to the big race, we hear "Teen Angel" (about a young girl dying in a car wreck), and finally, when Curt waits for his dream girl to call, he and we hear "Only You."

Virtually the entire film is narrativized by the music track, the stack of 45's spun by "the crude disc jockey," Wolfman Jack. The Wolfman's ability to sense what is going on in these teens' lives and to speak to teenagers' peculiar problems (simply by choosing the appropriate song) testifies to his role in the film and in the lives of so many American teenagers as a kind of mystical, omniscient authority. Like Santa Claus, he knows if they've been bad or good . . . like God, he is, as he unself-consciously remarks over the air, "everywhere."

Of at least equal importance is the continued appropriateness of the music itself; it, too, in the lives of these teenagers emerges as an indisputable narrativizing and authorizing force. In *American Graffiti*, as in so many teen films since its release in 1973, the soundtrack is designed to articulate precisely what teenagers feel they themselves can never express. It demarcates their generation not only from that of their parents, but from previous and subsequent generations of youth culture as well. But in the final analysis, however rebellious it feels at the time, the music is organized, orchestrated by disc jockeys and record company executives who are not teenagers.

Lucas's intention was to make some sort of comment on American youth on the edge of the Vietnam era, but *American Graffiti* is far too

lovingly Kennedyan to provide a broader, darker, angrier picture of what was shortly to come. Indeed, Curt, the film's most interesting character, has but one life's goal: to shake John F. Kennedy's hand. For him and his friends, these are the years of Camelot, when, for one "shining moment," being a teenager in America meant being part of a glorious—even if it turned out to be spurious—dream. That Curt's dream, as it would be for so many young people of his generation, is dashed within a year or so of this last fateful night of youth is a point saved only for the film's very strange postscript.

Like *Animal House*, closure in *American Graffiti* is a time to put the hijinks of youth aside. Like most teen films, both *Animal House* and *American Graffiti* are really about the end of youth, the impossibility of remaining young forever. As a result, both films end with strange and serious postscripts regarding the real future of fictive characters. In the closing title sequence of *American Graffiti*, we are told, for example, that Toad is missing-in-action in Vietnam. John, who "grows up" to become an anonymous car mechanic (not even the "Mickey Mantle of the greasepits" that his successor Fonzie would become on the very derivative *Happy Days*), is killed in a car accident with a drunk driver. Steve becomes (and this never fails to prompt the appropriate response from the audience) an insurance agent and Curt, the only character who gets out of town, is in Canada dodging the draft, writing successfully.

However gratuitous such an ending felt in 1973, especially given the rest of the movie and the overpoweringly positive soundtrack, such a moral is now, in retrospect, quintessentially Lucas. For Lucas, only Curt embraced the American Libertarian dream, thus only Curt got out of Modesto "alive." Indicatively, no postscript is provided for the young women. Even in the future, Lucas suggests that they are (still) peripheral, perhaps supportive but ultimately and most certainly (still) uninteresting.[13]

Nostalgia as Romance

At the end of the opening title sequence in *A Night in the Life of Jimmy Reardon* there is an allusion to Aldous Huxley that bears rather significantly on a number of recent teen nostalgia films. "Our goal

is to discover that we have always been where we ought to be," Huxley posits, "Unhappily we make that task exceedingly difficult for ourselves."

Such a sentiment characterizes the extremely popular teen pictures written, produced, and occasionally directed by ex-advertising executive John Hughes. *Sixteen Candles* (1984), *Pretty in Pink* (1986), *The Breakfast Club* (1985), *Some Kind of Wonderful* (1987), and *Ferris Bueller's Day Off* (1986) all defer to a nostalgia for 1930s screwball comedy and Capra-esque Libertarian populism. And through such an homage to the Depression era thirties—films that were embedded in and imbued with the ideologies of austerity and class struggle—Hughes's little dramas of class warfare end quite as Huxley predicts, with the triumph of individuality over an arbitrary social immobility.[14]

In *Pretty in Pink*, for example, we find a high school world dominated by social-class drawn cliques. When Andie, the quintessential Hughes outsider, falls for Blaine, a popular "richie," the rather rigid order of things begins to crumble. When Blaine asks her out, Steph, Blaine's arrogant richie friend, warns him that his stuck-up parents will never approve. That romance could displace the rigid social order (that empowers him, though he is clearly a creep) is beyond Steph's and Blaine's parents' imaginations. Regarding Blaine's pursuit of Andie, Steph says simply: "I think it's just stupid . . . it's pointless."

Blaine is, in his own words, "the crown prince of McDonaugh Electric." Andie is an unpopular eccentric who dresses in thrift store vogue despite or because of the galleria teen world around her. Their first date is, predictably, a disaster. Blaine's friends are openly hostile and Andie's one high school friend, the class clown Duckie, allows his jealousy to get the better of him. To assert his individuality—in the face of such resistance on both sides—Blaine asks Andie to the prom. But in the end, he backs out without so much as a phone call or an apology.

At the end of *Pretty in Pink*, though she feels jilted and humiliated, Andie decides to go to the prom anyway, alone. When she arrives, Duckie is there waiting for her, sort of dressed up and sure he's there to pick up the pieces. (Indeed, like Steph and apparently Blaine as well, he knew from the start that Andie's affair with a boy from a wealthy family would never work out.) When Duckie escorts Andie

into the gym, further suggesting the realization of his dreams, the subsequent sequence of shots sets up something altogether different: (1) a master shot of the prom; (2) a two-shot of Andie and Duckie; (3) a medium close shot of Steph (drunk and sad); (4) a medium close shot of Blaine looking at the camera; and (5) the repetition of shot #2, indicating that Andie and Duckie are what Blaine is looking at. We then cut to Blaine crossing the room, his progress intercut with shots of Andie clutching Duckie's hand. This is, for her, a moment of truth, a rite of passage.

Delaying the inevitable, Steph intercepts Blaine. But he is summarily rejected. "You couldn't buy her," Blaine bristles, "She thinks you're shit and deep down you know she's right." The issue of class that so dominated the rest of the film is rendered moot at the turn of such a phrase. So, by the time Blaine confronts Andie and Duckie, it is only her pride that stands in the way of true love.

As the third man out, Duckie steps aside. It is, after all, his role in the film to do so. "You told me you couldn't believe in somebody who didn't believe in you," Blaine confesses to Andie in what is a pretty typical Hollywood sentiment, "I've always believed in you. I just didn't believe in me." While she ponders her alternatives, he exits for the parking lot. Seconds later she joins him. The two embrace and as the camera pulls back to show them in full figure, we see them kiss. The screen then cuts to black and we hear the title song, an up-beat number sung in hypnotic monotone that invites us to shake our heads "yes" in approval at such an ending.

The ending of *Pretty in Pink* satisfies the conventions of romantic comedy. The social class obstructions to the (re)union of the desired and desirable couple are overcome. In what Northroup Frye terms comedy's "final festival,"[15] all the characters assemble to celebrate as a new order is installed—a new order that is decidedly feminine.

Jim Leach argues that the ideology of romantic comedy, i.e. the mystical prescience of the loser-outsider and *her* victory over a corrupt and corrupting society, engages a restoration and realization of the American ideal of a classless and egalitarian society.[16] Such a populism, such a democratic benevolence, coordinates a victory of romance over cynicism—a position "foolishly" clung to by Andie in *Pretty in Pink* throughout the course of the narrative.

David Shumway offers an interesting turn on such a reading of the genre. Positing that "romance is very often the receptacle of displacement, which is fitting for a term that has come to be almost a synonym for illusion," Shumway suggests that these films "mystify romance."[17] They are comic precisely because they are unbelievable.

The notion of a victory of the feminine—and we can read this as either a healthy or screwball course of events—allows us to better understand another of Hughes's populist teen films, *Some Kind of Wonderful*. Like *Pretty in Pink*, *Some Kind of Wonderful* focuses on a hapless outsider, this time a teenage boy named Keith, who, like Andie, falls for someone seemingly out of his class, in this case, the school's reigning heartthrob, Amanda Jones. The problematics of such a romance are made obvious in the opening credit sequence, as we see Keith working at a gas station intercut with shots of Amanda out riding in her boyfriend Harley's expensive sports car. The sequence ends as Harley and Amanda pull into the gas station for a fill-up. Like *Pretty in Pink*, the drama is reduced to simplistic class issues and once again we see a high school rigidly organized according to cliques that solely regard wealth in its division of society.

While Keith pines for Amanda, Wats, the film's female version of *Pretty in Pink*'s Duckie, longs for Keith to fall in love with her. From the start, she warns him to stay away from "the big money, cruel hearts society," to not "go roaming where [he doesn't] belong." But, of course, he needs to learn that lesson for himself. He ignores her advice, just as he fails to see that she loves him and that he loves her. When Keith, through weird luck, gets a date with Amanda—she's dumping Harley just as he asks her out—he runs to Wats with the "good" news. Immediately put on the defensive by Wats, he insists that Amanda's different. "You can't tell a book by its cover," he says. But Wats's comeback is far more convincing: "But you can tell how much it costs."

Harley, like Steph in *Pretty in Pink*, and like most richies in Hughes's films, is dissolute, bored, and heartless. When he invites Keith and Amanda to his party, he says to Keith: "It wouldn't be the weirdest thing in the world if we turned out to be friends." "Yes it would," Keith replies, and he's right. When Wats is told the story, she concurs: "Did I miss something—like a new world order?"

By the end of the film, Amanda is revealed to be different (as in better). She rejects Harley and his richie friends, but exits alone. As Wats knew all along, it was she who Keith always loved. Harley and his clique are left to be beaten up by Keith's new-found greaser friends. (As in *The Breakfast Club* and *Ferris Bueller's Day Off*, Hughes's heroes eventually transcend the rigid high school order and are befriended by delinquents who are really more like them than they or we had expected.) More importantly though, all three of the teenagers we care about turn out to be pretty terrific.

Though *Some Kind of Wonderful* inverts the ending of *Pretty in Pink*, it too insists on the clairvoyance and persistence of the feminine. But, as in so many romantic comedies, that the woman knows best does her little good through the course of the narrative. In both *Pretty in Pink* and *Some Kind of Wonderful*, the heroines must wait out high school, their entire adolescence, before they realize their desire. When "it" finally happens, it's a graduation in all kinds of ways. The message in virtually every one of Hughes's teen films is that true love is, for girls, at the far end of adolescence. It's just a matter of time. But for boys, at the far end of the youth culture they so dominate is adult commitment, nine-to-five work and family—in other words, a world dominated by women. For boys, the message is that youth is a desperate time, one which is "some kind of wonderful" precisely because it won't last.

Nostalgia as Deconstruction/Nostalgia as Hip

"The prevailing purpose of the American teen flick," writes Geoff Pevere, "is the defusing of any perceived threats to conventional order posed by the constant threat of teen transgression. Typically, these threats are channelled in a cathartic, temporary and largely harmless fashion, specifically into the clarion call of apolitical passions represented by [straight] sex, drugs and rock and roll." But though Pevere's argument speaks to the vast majority of fifties' teen movies, it imposes a cultural function on the teen film it no longer carries, a cultural function that is by now no longer necessary. Thus, "the systematic acknowledgement, exploitation and containment of the insurrectionary impulses of adolescence" that Pevere views as essential

to the teen film's ideological effect,[18] now refer to the very elements nostalgic teen films parody, catalogue, pastiche.

In Michael Lehmann's *Heathers* (1989), for example, we find "the insurrectionary impulse of adolescence" the focus of the film's black humor. Indeed, the very predictability and familiarity of the genre allows the teen audience not only to laugh at themselves, but to commune in the acknowledgment of a shared knowledge—a shared knowledge of the very idiocy of the media's re-presentation of them.

Thus, it is a joke that all the popular girls in the film are named Heather, that the new kid in town is a juvenile delinquent named Jason Dean (initials: J.D.), and that the film's heroine is a dark-haired good-girl named Veronica (as in the *Archie* comic books). The rest of the school—and this too is a joke on genre convention—is populated by irrelevant but easily recognizable types: geeks, fatsos, dopers, jocks, and the occasional greaser.

Heathers also features a multitude of allusions to popular television and film: *Adam 12*, *Leave it to Beaver*, *Gilligan's Island*, *Rock and Roll High School*, *Rebel Without a Cause*, and *River's Edge*. The audience then is meant to feel reassured by their shared expertise in the dubious art of their generation, reveling in the ever-so-passive hip of postmodern ennui. As a result, *Heathers* is all teen-pic pastiche: a teen film to end all teen films.

Heather Chandler, aka Heather 1, begins the film in firm control of the high school and of the narrative. In an early scene, she looks across the cafeteria at a nerd who, in abject fear of what her look could mean, responds by spitting up in his milk. "I'm worshipped here at Westerburg [High School]," she quips, "and I'm only a junior." Later, when Heather Duke (aka Heather 3) seizes control, Veronica asks: "Why do you have to be such a mega-bitch?," to which Heather responds, "Because I can."

The film depicts a series of murders faked as suicides all deliberately perpetrated by J.D. and witnessed and unwittingly accompliced by Veronica. Until the end of the film, it is J.D.'s keen awareness of the vagaries of teen authority that motivates the action. For example, when he tries to get back at Veronica, who tells him she's had enough after three killings, J.D. cleverly manipulates Heather Duke. "We don't need mushy togetherness [the new order proposed by a ridic-

ulous ex-hippie teacher]," he tells her, "We need a strong leader." With such an entreaty, Heather Duke is transformed, prompting Veronica to redundantly observe: "I cut off Heather Chandler's head and Heather Duke's has grown in its place."

Following Heather Duke's transformation, Veronica has a particularly troubling and vivid dream. In it, she and J.D. argue over yet another murder: Heather Duke's. Glibly concluding (in a typical bit of *Heathers* teen-speak) that her "teenage angst bullshit has a body count," Veronica tells him she wants out. "Tomorrow someone else's gonna take her place," she quips, "[and] that person could be me."

When all else fails, Veronica tries to reason with J.D. After three murders faked as suicides, she tells him, no one will believe in a fourth. But he is undaunted and provides the film's black comic payoff: "Society nods its head at any horror the American teenager can think to bring upon himself." And though this is her dream, Veronica, for once, is at a loss for words.

Later in the film, when J.D. proposes to blow up the school, he again tries to cull Veronica's support. "You want to clean the slate as much as I do," he tells her, "the only place different social types can get together is in heaven. People are going to look at the ashes of Westerburg and say, 'now there's a school that self-destructed not because society didn't care, but because the school was society.' " Though she basically agrees with him, by this point in the film she's heard enough and shoots him with his gun. That she "seizes the phallus" all too obviously signifies her decision to take control of the narrative.

Defeated, but still philosophical, J.D. reappears out in front of the school, much the worse for wear, to pass the mantle of authority to Veronica. "I'm thoroughly impressed," he says, "You really fucked me up pretty bad . . . You've got power. Power I didn't know you had. The slate is clean." With such an affirmation of her ability to seize the day, J.D. blows himself up and out of her life. Her face blackened by the explosion, her clothes in tatters—her appearance for the first time in the film not essentially perfect—she re-enters the high school and confronts Heather Duke. "Veronica," Heather cattily remarks, "you look like hell." "Well, I just got back," Veronica responds. Then, with a line that all but sums up the closure of virtually every teen

movie, Veronica pulls the ribbon (the symbol of authority in the film) from Heather's hair and quips, "Heather my love, there's a new sheriff in town."

From Romance to Ruin

While the postmodern pastiche of *Heathers* restores the thematic and ideological thrust of the conventional teen movie narrative, Francis Coppola's stylistically dense *Rumble Fish* problematizes such a dubious structuration of authority.

In *Rumble Fish*, the culturally significant teen film narrative—one that rewrites the history of youth culture into the conservative and reassuring formula of Hollywood melodrama, musical comedy, horror, and adventure—is dismantled and ultimately rendered moot. The postmodern effect in *Rumble Fish* is that in the end there is nothing save the failure of virtually every motion picture style—since they are, almost all of them, used at one point or another in the film—to explain away the hopelessness and bankruptcy of post-World War II America here epitomized and dramatized by bored and aimless youth.

The seemingly depthless, cool world of the film is presented in black-and-white, the "color" of realism. But what we see is hardly realistic. The film was shot on location in Tulsa, Oklahoma in 1982 where the S.E. Hinton novel, *Rumble Fish*, takes place some twenty-five years earlier. While this could suggest realism, nostalgia, even urban history in a more conventional movie, Coppola's interests lay in the creation of a pointedly anti-realist, ethereal, ahistorical space, frantically allusory to Expressionism and film noir while at the same time chronicling a familiar wild-teen romance. The score, composed and performed by ex-Police percussionist Stewart Copeland, bears a distinct reggae beat, hardly a reference to Tulsa circa 1960 or 1982.

In the rumble that basically opens the action in *Rumble Fish*, we find a model of the film's deconstructive thrust. Two tough boys, Rusty James and Biff Wilcox, face off down by the tracks. It's a familiar scenario, but Coppola purposefully foregoes an establishing shot or any semblance of visual continuity or theatrical blocking and staging to open up and delineate the scene. Instead, what we see is stylistically fascinating: complex, visceral, and formally decentering. Frenetic

cuts, skewed camera angles, and low key lighting (complementing the steam rising from the overheated city streets) highlight style as content, as an end in itself.

During the carefully choreographed and expressive fight scene—not unlike the rumble as dance in *West Side Story* or *Absolute Beginners*—the Motorcycle Boy (played by Mickey Rourke) arrives. He is from the start framed in a choker close-up, his head tilted to the side and looking just like Marlon Brando in the publicity stills for *The Wild One*.

"What is this," he asks, "another glorious fight for the kingdom?" Rusty James, who by this point has trounced Biff, looks up at his brother and away from his opponent. Biff then rises and guts Rusty James with a jagged piece of glass. The Motorcycle Boy's apparent ability to seize authority any time he feels like it paradoxically commences as his brother lies bleeding on the street.

The Motorcycle Boy's absence and then his presence on the scene at first appears to be an issue of some real importance. Without him, it is clear, there has been a total breakdown of authority on the streets. But with the Motorcycle Boy (as a kind of postmodern teen anti-hero), the binary opposition of presence and absence is effaced. When he is present, he's not all there; he's hard of hearing and he can't see colors. When he's gone, his legend remains significantly behind.

After the rumble scene, Rusty James and the Motorcycle Boy share a brotherly moment together. It is, for anyone who has ever taken an acting class, a familiar "method" exercise. It informs us in no uncertain terms that these actors are "doing" the method. As pure stylized performance, the scene tells us nothing about the characters though it tells us everything we need to know about the actors. Rather than use an acting style to prompt a narrative effect, Coppola reduces style to a code which is at once familiar (as a code), just as it is boring and meaningless.

Though the film is at once nostalgic and romantic, at the core of it all is a profound emptiness. Indeed, the brothers' relationship, which is the central focus of the narrative, is aptly summed up in the following dialogue:

> Motorcycle Boy (MB): Poor kid, looks like you're messed up all the
> time.

Rusty James (RJ): I'm OK. Let's go out and get a bite to eat.
MB: Hey.
RJ: What?
MB: Hey. (Pause) Hey.
RJ: What?
MB: Hey.
RJ: I'm all right man.
MB: Why?
RJ: Why what?
MB: Why?
RJ: Fuck.
MB: Hey, hey.
RJ: What?
MB: Why? Why?—No, no, no—Don't tell me fuck, fuck—Why? Why? Huh?
RJ: Let's go get something to eat.
MB: You can talk to me—why?
RJ: Why what? (exasperated) Why?
MB: Why are you fucked up all the time one way or another, huh?
RJ: I don't know.

Much of what's left of the narrative—in the face of so much style—is undercut by the refusal or inability of either potential hero, the Motorcycle Boy or Rusty James, to seize the day. In the absence of a functional hero (the dominant structure of authority in narrative in general) or the gangs (the organizing principle of teen street life), drugs fragment the leaderless teen world. When Rusty James gets set to fight Biff, for example, his nostalgic euphoria at the prospect of a rumble is tempered when he discovers that Biff is high on pills. Throughout, Rusty James laments how drugs ruined the gangs, how drugs supplanted an authority he rather yearns for.

Late in the film, as Rusty James recovers from yet another brutal beating, the Motorcycle Boy shares his brother's lament. In a rueful, ambiguous speech set under a bridge and blocked as if it were on stage, as if it were a payoff scene in a film, the Motorcycle Boy looks to the future: "The gangs will come back," he says, "people will persist at joining things . . . Once they get the dope off the streets, you'll see the gangs come back—if you live that long." But at the core

of his argument is a profound ennui. Indeed, the Motorcycle Boy concludes that the gangs disappeared because youth itself got boring.

The Motorcycle Boy's glib analysis of a generation born to follow underscores his refusal to be a hero. While so many teen films portray an unlikely youth who through fate or chance or just desserts becomes a hero, the Motorcycle Boy seems a likely candidate, but he just wants to rest in peace.

Near the end of the film, in a vain attempt to rescue the Motorcycle Boy, Rusty James tracks his brother to a magazine store in downtown Tulsa. On the way, he passes graffiti scrawled on a street sign that reads: "The Motorcycle Boy Reigns"—a sign we see in the opening tracking shot and at the very end of the film. In all three cases, the graffiti is written on an arrow pointing in the opposite direction from the movement of the camera.

Inside the store, we see the Motorcycle Boy perusing a magazine in which there is a photograph of him with the caption "today's youth." Uncomfortable with the prospect of an increased notoriety, the Motorcycle Boy wants the story kept quiet. But Rusty James doesn't get why. The conversation that follows articulates the distance between them and characterizes the Motorcycle Boy's peculiar brand of anomie:

> MB: I'd just as soon stay a neighborhood novelty if it's all the same
>   to you—I'm tired of all this pied piper bullshit.
> RJ: The pied piper man—the guy with the flute—the guy in the movie.
> MB: (sarcastic) They'd all follow me to the river and jump in.
> RJ: (misreading his brother's tone, in earnest and with pride) They
>   probably would.
> MB: If you're going to lead people, you have to have some place to
>   go.

Unlike Jim Stark in *Rebel Without a Cause*, who is so conflicted he desperately wants someone to tell him what to do, the Motorcycle Boy is so bored as he just wants someone to take him out. He is Tulsa's best fighter, lover, pool player, and gang leader. He's a poet, and now I'm quoting from the film, "a prince in exile," "a hero miscast in a play," but it isn't close to being enough. For both, being

a teen hero is a lonely place. But while Jim desperately wants to grow up, the Motorcycle Boy has seen enough to know better.

In the novel, Rusty James describes his brother as follows: "He had an expressionless face . . . he saw things other people couldn't see, and laughed when nothing was funny. He had strange eyes—they made me think of a two-way mirror. Like you could feel somebody on the other side watching you, but the only reflection was your own."[19] Steve, Rusty James's nerd sidekick warns his friend: "if you hang around [the Motorcycle Boy] very long you won't believe in anything."[20] Of course he's right.

While the film is told in the third person—in the sense that an omniscient camera reveals the story—the novel is narrated in the first person by Rusty James. Much of the novel attends to his inability to fathom what is going on around him. But Hinton's game with narration and narrative is not only complex, it is also contradictory. The novel is framed by two scenes on the beach, set well after the Motorcycle Boy's death, as Rusty James finally rejects his brother's once seductive authority. In doing so, the novel concludes with Rusty James's transition into adulthood. His growth as a character is essential to the drama that precedes it and centers us as readers.

No such frame, and no such point-of-view strategy, is present in the film. Rusty James is not only not the narrator, he is little more than a sidekick, a buffoon, Little John to the Motorcycle Boy's Robin Hood, a dutiful rodent to his brother's Pied Piper. The film is primarily about the Motorcycle Boy, a character about whom, in a classic narrative sense, there is very little to say. To an extent, closure concerns Rusty James's embrace of the lesson his brother('s death) has taught him. But what is that lesson? He never understood anything the Motorcycle Boy said when he was alive and he certainly never understood what his brother signified.

In the end of the film, Rusty James exits to nowhere on his brother's (we gather stolen) motorcycle (the phallic symbol of power and authority in how many teen movies?). But should he return, he has no message, no boon, no lesson, nothing.

Rumble Fish so deeply problematizes the teen film narrative that the familiar codes of the genre and of youth culture as we have come to know it through the genre end up revealing a world in which no

institutional or cultural authority can convince, can close off the narrative. The film insists that we've already seen it all, that any ending would be anti-climactic, inconsistent, unsatisfying.

By the end of the film, the strong and silent, anomic hero not only appears to be suicidal, he accomplishes his goal (pointedly, and anti-climactically, offscreen). The benevolent cop of *Rebel Without a Cause* is transformed into the imposing, authoritarian Officer Patterson, whose role it seems is to help the Motorcycle Boy realize his death wish. Cassandra, one of the two female leads, is a drug addict, and while she seems at first to be a significant character as well as metaphor, by the mid-point of the narrative she vanishes altogether. Patty, Rusty James's girlfriend, dumps him and takes up with Smokey, who remarks (to Rusty James) that "it's no big deal." The father doesn't quit drinking. The mother never returns. In the end, Rusty James is still a teenager, lost in a world he may never adequately understand. Though the film presents the decadence of institutional authority and the subsequent search for a viable and traditional alternative (that typifies the genre), such a search is thwarted at every turn. The film ends unambiguously in boredom, suicide, hopelessness.

If the heart of *Rumble Fish*'s peculiar postmodernism is a however unintentional undermining of narrative pleasure (of the *jouissance* of generic fiction), then is such an obstruction to pleasure (of repetition, of genre conventions, of binary oppositions, of the sublime) somehow progressive? nihilist? experimental? avant-garde? Is the rejection of the conformity of adulthood and of the teen film in *Rumble Fish* somehow hopeful?

I think the answer is no. Questions regarding whether or not narrative pleasure is good or bad are subsumed by the film's apocalyptic mindset, positing that on the one hand anything goes, on the other, that pleasure isn't real, that pleasure isn't attainable anyway. If all narrative attends to a struggle for control (and I think it does) and the sublime is that moment when all the pain and confusion is resolved, *Rumble Fish* depicts how genre narratives these days fail to resolve the ideological contradictions inherent to contemporary society.

While most teen narratives are restorative and offer a rather complete closure, *Rumble Fish* coolly testifies to the ways in which such

narratives are false and neat. The depthless and cool world of Coppola's *Rumble Fish* is revealed in the shift from parody to pastiche, in the anti-ideology of boredom, in the calm before the storm: the last stop on the road to ruin.

Parting Glances

"Should I go to college?
Or Should I join the service?
Thinking about the future
Just makes me nervous.
It's a complex world
And sometimes I feel like
A ch-ch-ch-ch-chimpanzee."[21]

In a review of Oliver Stone's *JFK* (1991), Andrew Kopkind offers the following alternative explanation for the present popularity of the nostalgia film. "The generation of Americans for whom the [Kennedy] assassination was the first traumatic world event is now coming into early middle age. It is a point when people for the first time feel they have 'arrived' somewhere in life, and they may look back to see the landmarks that led them to where they are. They think of television shows they saw as teenagers, they remember their partner at the senior prom, they recall leaving home, finding a first job, starting a family."[22]

Though Kopkind's argument offers the flip-side of Jameson's—positing nostalgia as an historical project (albeit in the quintessential eighties' soul-searching, self-discovery mode)—he shares with Jameson an awareness of his generation's sense of self-importance. It is, after all, the images of their youth that have come back to the future. And for the teen film which is now dominated by these images, the history lesson (if there is one) is far different for those late-thirty-and-forty-something than it is for the teenagers at whom these films are ostensibly targeted.

The dark side of such a nostalgic project is that teenagers today are denied the very community these films insist once existed. For this generation of teenagers, the present is dominated by images and narratives of their parents' youth. These largely reassuring journeys

into the past are plenty diverting, but may well leave today's youth wholly unprepared to think seriously about the future in any terms other than those they've already seen on the big screen.

The future, all things considered, promises to be a terrifying place. As Will Baker concludes in his gloomy assessment of global youth: "To be young at this time is definitely not very heavenly. It is to be confused by incessant broadcasts of conflicting propaganda, exploited as cheap labor [Baker's quintessential global youth is "that pretty young student whose future is serving you hamburgers at McDonalds for eighteen cents an hour"],[23] targeted or seduced as a 'market,' educated and exhorted as saviors of one's country, picked up and interrogated, sometimes beaten and shot."[24]

A recent UNESCO study echoes Baker's reality check. "The key words in the experience of the young," the study concludes, "are going to be: 'scarcity,' 'unemployment,' 'underemployment,' 'ill-employment,' 'anxiety,' 'defensiveness,' 'pragmatism,' and even 'subsistence' and 'survival' itself."[25]

Here in the United States, the teen drop-out, pregnancy, crime and unemployment rates continue to rise. More alarming still is the teen suicide rate. In 1987, for example, 1901 teenagers killed themselves. That's eighteen out of every 100,000; twice the rate from 1970.[26]

Given such alarming social conditions, the teen film's increasing self-parody and self-reflexivity—in other words, its penchant for nostalgia—seems hardly surprising. The cultural function of the teen film has always been primarily one of reassurance. But in the years to come, we need to ask not only whether such reassurance is in bad faith, but whether or not (for such dark times) it will be enough?

Notes

Introduction

1.   Will Baker, "The Global Teenager," *Whole Earth Review* (Winter, 1989), p. 3.

2.   Don DeLillo, *Great Jones Street* (NY: Vintage, 1989), p. 132.

3.   Baker, "Global Teenager," p. 2.

4.   Kevin Kelley, "Selling the World: Mouseketeers to Marketeers," *Whole Earth Review (Winter, 1989), p. 36.*

5.   Theodor W. Adorno, *Prisms*, trans. Samuel and Shierry Weber (London: Neville Spearman, 1967), p. 128.

6.   Theodor W. Adorno, "Culture Industry Reconsidered," trans. Anson G. Rabinbach, *New German Critique*, vol. 6 (Fall, 1975), p. 17.

7.   Simon Frith paraphrasing Adorno's "culture industry" argument, in *Sound Effects: Youth, Leisure and the Politics of Rock 'n' Roll* (NY: Pantheon, 1981), p. 57.

8.   Guy Debord, *Society of the Spectacle* (Detroit: Red and Black, 1977), paragraph 17.

9.   Debord, *Society of the Spectacle*, paragraph 32.

10.   Theodor W. Adorno, "On Popular Music," in *On Record: Rock, Pop and the Written Word*, ed. Simon Frith and Andrew Goodwin (NY: Pantheon, 1990), p. 312.

11.   Debord, *Society of the Spectacle*, paragraph 218.

12.   *The Challenge of Youth*, ed. Erik H. Erikson (NY: Doubleday, 1965) is a collection of essays on youth culture first presented at the Tamiment Institute Conference in 1961, then published in the Winter 1961/1962 issue of *Daedalus*.

13.   Erik H. Erikson, "Editor's Preface," in *The Challenge of Youth*, p. viii.

14.   Dick Hebdige, *Subculture: The Meaning of Style* (London: Methuen, 1979), p. 17.

15.   Hebdige, *Subculture*.

16.   Hebdige, *Subculture*, p. 167.

17. Stuart Hall, "Culture, the Media and the 'Ideological Effect,' " in *Mass Communication and Society*, ed. James Curran (NY: Sage, 1979).

18. Hall, "Culture, the Media and the 'Ideological Effect.' "

19. Hebdige paraphrasing Hall in *Subculture: The Meaning of Style*, p. 85.

20. Frith, *Sound Effects: Youth, Leisure and the Politics of Rock 'n' Roll*, p. 196.

21. Stuart Hall and Paddy Whannel, "The Young Audience," in *On Record: Rock, Pop and the Written Word*, p. 29.

22. Paul Corrigan and Simon Frith, "The Politics of Youth Culture," *Working Papers in Cultural Studies*, nos. 7/8 (Summer, 1975), p. 237.

23. Walter Benjamin, "Theses on the Philosophy of History," in *Illuminations*, ed. Hanna Arendt, trans. Harry Zohn (NY: Harcourt, Brace and World, 1968).

24. Max Horkheimer and Theodor W. Adorno, *Dialectic of Enlightenment*, trans. John Cumming (NY: Herder and Herder, 1972), p. 163.

25. Frith, *Sound Effects: Youth, Leisure and the Politics of Rock 'n' Roll*, p. 129.

Chapter One—The End of the World (as we know it)

1. *The title of the opening chapter in Edith Fass, The Damned and the Beautiful: American Youth in the 1920's* (NY: Oxford University Press, 1977).

2. Kenneth Keniston, *The Uncommitted: Alienated Youth in American Society* (NY: Harcourt, Brace and World, 1965), p. 197.

3. Keniston, *The Uncommitted*, p. 191.

4. Keniston, *The Uncommitted*, pp. 84–103.

5. Keniston, *The Uncommitted*, p. 3.

6. Keniston, *The Uncommitted*, p. 391.

7. Robin Wood, *Hollywood from Vietnam to Reagan* (NY: Columbia University Press, 1086), p. 168.

8. Andrew Britton, "Blissing Out: The Politics of Reaganite Entertainment," *Movie*, vols. 31/32 (1985), p. 19.

9. Gavin Smith, "Pensées: Pretty Vacant in Pink," *Film Comment*, vol. 23, no. 4 (July–August, 1987), p. 70.

10. Indeed, this is the dominant line of argument in what I have termed the "American ("psycho-social") School" in youth cultural study: Keniston, Bettleheim, Erikson, Parsons, Denney, and Eisenstadt.

11. The title of a short story by Joyce Carol Oates about a teenage girl breaking away from her mother: "Where Are You Going, Where Have You

Been?," *The Short Story: Thirty Masterpieces* (NY: St. Martins, 1987), pp. 440–456.

12. Robert K. Merton as cited by Eric and Mary Josephson in the introduction to *Man Alone*, ed. Eric and Mary Josephson (NY: Dell, 1962), p. 14.

13. Chip Brown, "Friday the 13th Murder Leaves Town Fearful of Satanism," the *Oregonian*, November 4, 1990, p. A32.

14. Charles Leerhorn, "This Year's Model," *Newsweek* (special edition: "The New Teens: What Makes Them Different?") (Summer/Fall 1990), p. 47.

15. Elliot Leyton, *Hunting Humans: The Rise of the Modern Multiple Murderer* (Toronto: McLelland and Stewart, 1986), p. 26.

16. Bryan Bruce, "The Edge," *CineAction*, no. 12 (April, 1988), p. 37. (Leyton makes the same point in *Hunting Humans*; on p. 27.)

17. Bruce, "The Edge," p. 37.

18. Smith, "Pensées," p. 70.

19. Norman Mailer, *The White Negro* (San Francisco: City Lights, 1957).

20. William Whyte, *The Organization Man* (NY: Anchor, 1957). Whyte argues that postwar society discouraged initiative and rewarded conformity, that the concept of subsuming the self to the corporate team (the essence of the organization man philosophy) undermined the American male ideal.

21. David Riesman, *The Lonely Crowd* (New Haven: Yale University Press, 1950). "Other-directedness" was the psychological foundation of the organization man. And it is worth adding here that Riesman, like Whyte, lamented the passing of the rugged, individualist male. For Riesman, "other-directedness" involves an e- or de-masculinization of the culture. "Today it is the softness of men," Riesman writes, "rather than the hardness of material that calls on talent and opens new channels of social mobility" (p. 127).

22. Barbara Ehrenreich, *The Hearts of Men: American Dreams and the Flight from Commitment* (NY: Anchor, 1983), pp. 14–28.

23. Bruno Bettleheim, "The Problem of Generations," in *The Challenge of Youth*, ed. Erik H. Erikson (NY: Doubleday, 1965), pp. 89–90.

24. Bettleheim, "The Problem of Generations," p. 92.

25. David Gelman, "A Much Riskier Passage," *Newsweek* (special edition: "The New Teens: What Makes Them Different?"), p. 15.

26. Erik Erikson, "Youth, Fidelity and Diversity," in *The Challenge of Youth*, p. 24.

27. Erich Fromm, *Man For Himself* (NY: Rinehart, 1947) and *The Sane Society* (NY: Rinehart, 1955); Erich Kahler, *The Tower and the Abyss: An*

Inquiry Into the Transformation of the Individual (NY: Braziller, 1957); Fritz Pappenheim, *The Alienation of the Modern Man* (NY: Monthly Review, 1959); Murray Levin, *The Alienated Voter* (NY: Holt, Rinehart and Winston, 1960); C. Wright Mills, *The Power Elite* (NY: Oxford University Press, 1956); David Riesman, *The Lonely Crowd*; Paul Goodman, *Growing Up Absurd* (NY: Random House, 1960); William Whyte, *The Organization Man*; Daniel Bell, *The End of Ideology* (Glencoe, Ill: Free Press, 1960); William Kornhauser, *The Politics of Mass Society* (Glencoe, Ill: Free Press, 1958), and Kenneth Keniston, *The Uncommitted: Alienated Youth in American Society*.

28. Eric and Mary Josephson, "Introduction," in *Man Alone*, pp. 12–13.

29. Emile Durkheim, *The Division of Labor in Society*, trans. W.D. Hall (NY: Free Press, 1985).

30. Philip Wylie, *Generation of Vipers* (NY: Farrar and Rinehart, 1946).

31. "The restoration of the father"—the re-emergence of the American male—is a key theme in both Andrew Britton and Robin Wood's work on the new American cinema. See Britton, "Blissing Out: The Politics of Reaganite Entertainment" and Wood, *Hollywood from Vietnam to Reagan*.

32. For a more extensive discussion of *Return of the Jedi* see Jon Lewis, "*Return of the Jedi*: A Situationist Perspective," *Jump Cut*, no. 30 (1984), pp. 3–6.

33. Ehrenreich, *The Hearts of Men*, p. 57.

34. Smith, "Pensées," p. 71.

35. Charles Ricks as cited by Geoff Mungham and Geoff Pearson in "Introduction: Troubled Youth, Troubling World," in *Working Class Youth Culture*, ed. Geoff Mungham and Geoff Pearson (London: Routledge and Kegan Paul, 1976), p. 9.

36. Kenneth Keniston, "Social Change and Youth in America," in *The Challenge of Youth*, p. 216.

Chapter Two: The Path of the Damned

1. Vincent Bugliosi, *Helter Skelter* (NY: Norton, 1974), p. 388.

2. As with much of what I have to say about Manson, here I owe a debt to an as yet unpublished paper: Eric Patterson, "Charles Manson's Family: Some Speculations About Its Organization and Development."

3. Bugliosi, *Helter Skelter*, p. 415. (The parenthetical digression is mine.)

4. Ed Sanders, *The Family* (NY: Avon, 1971), p. 151.

5. Here Patterson echoes Steven Roberts, "One Man's Family," *New York Times Magazine*, January 4, 1970, pp. 24–29.

6. Hunter Thompson, *Fear and Loathing in Las Vegas* (NY: Warner, 1971), pp. 178–179.

7. Thompson, *Fear and Loathing*, p. 178.

8. William L. O'Neill, *Coming Apart: An Informal History of America in the 1960's* (NY: Times Books, 1971), p. 264.

9. O'Neill, *Coming Apart*, pp. 263–264.

10. Bugliosi, *Helter Skelter*, pp. 461–462.

11. Bugliosi, *Helter Skelter*, p. 489.

12. Daniel and Judith Baskin Offer, *From Teenage to Young Manhood: A Psychological Study* (NY: Basic Books, 1975), pp. 4–5.

13. Dick Hebdige, *Subculture: The Meaning of Style* (London: Methuen, 1979) and *Hiding in the Light: On Images and Things* (NY: Routledge, 1989); Stuart Hall, Chas Crichter, Tony Jefferson, John Clarke, and Brian Roberts, *Policing the Crisis: Mugging, the State and Law and Order* (NY: Holmes and Meier, 1978) and Hall, "Deviancy, Politics and the Media," in *Deviance and Social Control*, ed. Paul Rock and Mary McIntosh (London: Tavistock, 1974); John Clarke, "Style" and "The Skinheads and the Magical Recovery of Working Class Community" in *Resistance Through Rituals*, ed. Stuart Hall, John Clarke, Tony Jefferson, and Brian Roberts (London: Hutchinson, 1976); and Phil Cohen, "Subcultural Conflict and Working Class Community," *Working Papers in Cultural Studies*, no. 2 (Spring, 1972).

14. Antonio Gramsci's theory of hegemony as cited by Hebdige in *Subculture: The Meaning of Style*, pp. 15–16.

15. Travis Hirschi, *Causes of Delinquency* (Berkeley: University of California Press, 1970), p. 26.

16. Mailer as cited by Hebdige, *Subculture: The Meaning of Style*, p. 3.

17. Kathie Dobie citing John B. Waller and some startling statistics from the Center for the Prevention of Interpersonal Violence, in "Growing Up With Violence," *Vogue* (December, 1990), p. 313.

18. Anthony Burgess, "Introduction: *A Clockwork Orange* ReSucked," in *A Clockwork Orange* (NY: Norton, 1988), p. vii.

19. Burgess, "Introduction," p. viii.

20. Burgess, "Introduction," p. x.

21. Burgess, "Introduction," p. viii.

22. Anthony Burgess, *A Clockwork Orange*, pp. 35–59.

23. Burgess, *Clockwork Orange*, p. 208.

24. Burgess, Clockwork Orange, p. 217.

25. Burgess, *Clockwork Orange*, p. 218.

26. Jerry Farber, *The Student As Nigger* (NY: Simon and Schuster, 1969), p. 92.

27. For a more detailed reading of the film, see Jon Lewis, "The Shifting Camera Point-of-View and Model of Language in Frederick Wiseman's *High School*," *Quarterly Review of Film Studies*, vol. 7, no. 1 (Winter, 1982), pp. 69–78.

28. Fredelle B. Maynard, "The Minds of High School Seniors," in *Generation Rap*, ed. Gene Stanford (NY: Dell, 1971), pp. 117–118.

29. Maynard, "Minds of High School Seniors," pp. 121–122.

30. Maynard, "Minds of High School Seniors, p. 121.

31. Richard Staehling, "The Truth About Teen Movies," in *The Kings of the B's*, ed. Todd McCarthy and Charles Flynn (NY: Dutton, 1975), p. 221.

32. Paul Goodman, "Moral Youth in an Immoral Society," in *Generation Rap*, pp. 73–74.

33. Farber, *Student as Nigger*, p. 35.

34. Kaspar Naegele, "Youth and Society: Some Observations," in *The Challenge of Youth*, p. 67.

35. The term "cinema of conservative reassurance" is Andrew Britton's. See "Blissing Out: The Politics of Reaganite Entertainment," *Movie*, vols. 31/32 (1985).

36. C. Wright Mills, "On Mass Society," in *Man Alone*, ed. Eric and Mary Josephson (NY: Dell, 1962), p. 270.

37. Michel Foucault, *Discipline and Punish: The Birth of the Prison*, trans. Alan Sheridan (NY: Pantheon, 1977).

38. Allan Bloom, *The Closing of the American Mind: How Higher Education Has Failed Democracy and Impoverished the Souls of Today's Students* (NY: Simon and Schuster, 1987).

39. E.D. Hirsch, Jr., "Cultural Literacy," *The American Scholar* (Spring, 1983), p. 162.

40. E.D. Hirsch, Jr., *Cultural Literacy: What America Needs to Know* (Boston: Houghton-Mifflin, 1987).

41. Geoff Mungham and Geoff Pearson, "Introduction: Troubled Youth, Troubling World," in *Working Class Youth Culture*, ed. Geoff Mungham and Geoff Pearson (London: Routledge and Kegan Paul, 1976), p. 9.

42. Marty Jezer, *The Dark Ages: Life in the United States, 1945–1960* (Boston: South End, 1982), p. 237.

43. Paul Goodman, *Growing Up Absurd* (NY: Random House, 1960), p. 11.

Chapter Three—The Way of the Beautiful

1. *Alfred C. Kinsey, Wardell B. Pomeroy, and Clyde E. Martin, Sexual Behavior in the Human Male* (Philadelphia: W.B. Saunders, 1948) and Alfred C. Kinsey, Wardell B. Pomeroy, Clyde E. Martin, and Paul H. Gebhard, *Sexual Behavior in the Human Female* (Philadelphia: W.B. Saunders, 1953).

2. William H. Masters and Virginia E. Johnson, *Human Sexual Response* (Boston: Little, Brown, 1966), pp. 301–302.

3. Vance Packard, *The Sexual Wilderness: The Contemporary Upheaval in Male-Female Relationships*, (NY: David McKay, 1968), pp. 13–14.

4. Packard, *The Sexual Wilderness*, p. 17.

5. Packard, *The Sexual Wilderness*, pp. 35–45.

6. Bruno Bettleheim, "The Problem of Generations," in *The Challenge of Youth*, ed. Erik H. Erikson (NY: Doubleday, 1965), pp. 81–83.

7. Margaret Mead, *Male and Female* (NY: Mentor, 1964), p. 216.

8. Angela McRobbie and Jenny Garber, "Girls and Subcultures," in *Resistance Through Rituals*, ed. Stuart Hall, John Clarke, Tony Jefferson, and Brian Roberts (London: Hutchinson, 1976), p. 209.

9. McRobbie, "Settling Accounts With Subcultures: A Feminist Critique," p. 80.

10. McRobbie and Garber, "Girls and Subcultures," p. 220.

11. It is important to note here that Hebdige virtually ignores gender issues in *Subculture: The Meaning of Style* (London: Methuen, 1979).

12. McRobbie and Garber, "Girls and Subcultures," p. 221.

13. Packard, *The Sexual Wilderness*, pp. 162, 203, 512.

14. Aaron Haas, *Teenage Sexuality* (NY: MacMillan, 1979), p. 66.

15. Ned Zeman, "The New Rules of Courtship," *Newsweek* (special edition: "The New Teens: What Makes Them Different?") (Summer/Fall, 1990), p. 27. It is worth adding here that, though Packard was hardly a careful researcher—in his day he was labeled a "popularist"—he at least surveyed young adults from a variety of geographic regions and economic backgrounds. The study cited by Zeman was conducted by the Urban Institute and focused only on urban teenagers. That young people grow up faster in the city is a commonly held assumption, one that seems valid to me.

16. E.J. Roberts, *Family Life and Sexual Learning* (Boston: Population Education, 1978).

17. Haas, *Teenage Sexuality*, p. 175.

18. Michael Scofield, *The Sexual Behaviour of Young People* (London: Longmans, 1965).

19. It is worth digressing here again to Robin Wood's *Hollywood from Vietnam to Reagan* (NY: Columbia University Press, 1986). More and more the threat to order and hegemony comes from a supernatural source—more often than not, in the form of demonic possession. As Wood argues, this is part of an ongoing attempt to stipulate that evil in contemporary society is not what men do, but what is done to them.

20. "The Terror of Pleasure" is the title of an essay on the contemporary horror film by Tania Modelski, anthologized in *Studies in Entertainment*, ed. Tania Modleski (Bloomington: Indiana University Press, 1986). Though most of the essay attends to the mass culture/high culture—postmodernism/modernism—debate, Modleski aptly characterizes the ambiguous and ambivalent relationship these films have with their audience. On page 161, for example, Modleski writes: "*Halloween* and *Friday the 13th* . . . adopt the point-of-view of the slasher, placing the spectator in the position of an unseen nameless presence which, to the audience's great glee, annihilate, one by one their screen surrogates." Such an "anti-narcissistic identification," Modleski concludes, delights audiences in the very act of frustrating desire, of blocking pleasure.

21. This, like *WarGames* and *The Unbelievable Truth*, seems a consequence of a communal nuclear anxiety. The Biblical scale of things—the themes of retribution and cleaning the slate—seems unmistakably apocalyptic.

22. Brenda O. Daly, "Laughing *With*, or Laughing *At* the Young Adult Romance," *English Journal* (October, 1989), p. 51.

23. Daly, "Laughing *With*," p. 58.

24. Northrop Frye, *The Secular Scripture: A Study of the Structure of Romance* (Cambridge, MA: Harvard University Press, 1978).

25. Here I am paraphrasing the pivotal question in Daly's essay. See "Laughing *With*," p. 55.

26. Kim Kennedy, *In-Between Love* (NY: Warner, 1985) as cited by Daly, "Laughing *With*," pp. 56–57.

27. Angela McRobbie, *Feminism and Youth Culture: From Jackie to Just Seventeen* (Cambridge, MA: Unwin Hyman, 1990).

28. Barbara Bradby, "Do-Talk and Don't Talk: The Division of the Subject in Girl Group Music," in *On Record: Rock, Pop and the Written Word*, ed. Simon Frith and Andrew Goodwin (NY: Pantheon, 1990), p. 366.

29. Daly, "Laughing *With*," p. 53.

30. William Asher as cited by Richard Staehling, "The Truth About Teen Movies," in *The Kings of the B's*, ed. Todd McCarthy and Charles Flynn (NY: Dutton, 1975).

31. As Hebdige argues in *Subculture: The Meaning of Style*, "There is an ideological significance to every signification" (p. 13). Style, then, for Hebdige, is youth's instinctive (if oblique) way to express its autonomy, its difference—the very things that *Grease* insists are irrelevant.

32. Though its style and tone suggest otherwise, *Fast Times At Ridgemont High* is altogether faithful to Cameron Crowe's non-fiction, first-person account of a year in the life of a Southern California high school. See Cameron Crowe, *Fast Times at Ridgemont High* (NY: Simon and Schuster, 1981).

33. There is one significant exception worth noting here: *36 Fillette* (Catherine Breillat, 1988). Modeled after the male-virgin teen films in the U.S., this French teen movie provides almost two hours' worth of tease and ends with a very sour pay-off (not unlike Golan and Globus's *The Last American Virgin*).

34. Wood, *Hollywood from Vietnam to Reagan*, pp. 216–221.

35. Wood, *Hollywood from Vietnam to Reagan*, p. 216.

36. Recent teen films by and large support the growing current of anti-intellectualism in the United States. *Revenge of the Nerds*, offers a potential antidote; indeed, it is, despite itself, an important, maybe even progressive film.

37. Packard, *The Sexual Wilderness*, p. 55.

38. J.D. Salinger, *The Catcher in the Rye* (NY: Bantam, 1968), p. 63.

Chapter Four—The Struggle For Fun

1. Stuart Hall and Paddy Whannel, "The Young Audience," in *On Record: Rock, Pop and the Written Word*, (ed. Simon Frith and Andrew Goodwin (NY: Pantheon, 1990).

2. Angela McRobbie, "Settling Accounts With Subcultures: A Feminist Critique," p. 72.

3. Simon Frith, *Sound Effects: Youth, Leisure and the Politics of Rock 'n' Roll* (NY: Pantheon, 1981), p. 47.

4. Simon Frith, "Rock and the Politics of Memory," in *The Sixties Without Apology*, ed. Sohnya Sayres, Anders Stephanson, Stanley Aronowitz, and Fredric Jameson (Minneapolis: University of Minnesota Press, 1984), p. 72.

5. Frith, "Rock and the Politics of Memory," p. 60.

6. Drew Hayward citing Julien Temple, in *The Beginners Guide to Absolute Beginners* (London: Corgi, 1986), p. 110.

7. Colin MacInnes, *Absolute Beginners* (NY: Dutton, 1985), p. 10.

8. J.D. Salinger, *The Catcher in the Rye* (NY: Bantam, 1968), p. 213.

9. An allusion to a famous poem by Emily Dickinson that characterizes insanity as a social rather than psychological problem: "Much madness is divinest sense—/To a discerning eye—Much sense—the starkest madness—/ 'Tis the majority—/In this, as All, prevail—/Assent—and you are sane—/Demur—you're straightaway dangerous—/And handled with a chain." See *American Poetry*, ed. Gary Wilson Allen, Walter B.Rideout, and James K. Robinson (NY: Harper and Row, 1965), p. 538.

10. Hayward citing MacInnes, *The Beginners Guide*, p. 83.

11. MacInnes, *Absolute Beginners*, p. 23.

12. MacInnes, *Absolute Beginners*, p. 24.

13. MacInnes, *Absolute Beginners*, p. 64.

14. MacInnes, *Absolute Beginners*, p. 194.

15. Frith, *Sound Effects: Youth, Leisure and the Politics of Rock 'n' Roll*, p. 220.

16. Richard Barnes, *Mods!* (London: Eel Pie, 1979), p. 15.

17. Frith, *Sound Effects: Youth, Leisure and the Politics of Rock 'n' Roll*, p. 247.

18. Dick Hebdige, "The Meaning of Mod," in *Resistance Through Rituals*, ed. Stuart Hall, John Clarke, Tony Jefferson, and Brian Roberts (London: Hutchinson, 1976), p. 88.

19. Here Hebdige is posing an argument about subcultural ideology by alluding to Louis Althusser, "Ideology and Ideological State Apparatuses (Notes Towards Investigation)," in *Lenin and Philosophy*, trans. Ben Brewster (NY: Monthly Review, 1971), pp. 127–186. The passage of importance here reads: "Ideology represents the imaginary relationship of individuals to the real conditions of their existence" (p. 162).

20. Hebdige, "The Meaning of Mod," p. 93.

21. Hebdige, "The Meaning of Mod," p. 90.

22. Frith, "Rock and the Politics of Memory," p. 63.

23. Frith, "Rock and the Politics of Memory," p. 60.

24. Frith, *Sound Effects: Youth, Leisure and the Politics of Rock 'n' Roll*, p. 134.

25. Within a year of the release of *Privilege*, the Who produced "Tommy," a rock opera about a deaf, dumb, and blind boy who is miraculously cured and becomes an authoritarian pop-messiah. At the end, Tommy, like Stephen Shorter is rejected by his fans as capriciously and passionately as they had first embraced him.

26. Don DeLillo, *Great Jones Street* (NY: Vintage, 1989), p. 1.

27. DeLillo, *Great Jones Street*, p. 105.

28. DeLillo, *Great Jones Street*, p. 144.

29. DeLillo, *Great Jones Street*, p. 124.

30. DeLillo, *Great Jones Street*, p. 194.

31. For a more complete reading of the film, see Jon Lewis, "Purple Rain: Music Video Comes of Age," *Jump Cut*, no. 30 (1984), pp. 1, 22, 43.

32. E. Ann Kaplan, "Feminism/Oedipus/Postmodernism: The Case of MTV," in *Postmodernism and Its Discontents*, ed. E. Ann Kaplan (NY: Verso, 1988), p. 37.

33. Nell Bernstein, "The Sex Queen May Appeal Most to Women," the *Oregonian*, August 24, 1990, p. D7.

34. Madonna as cited by Vicki Wooods in "Madonna Holds Court," *Vogue* (May, 1990), p. 345.

35. Lawrence Grossberg, "MTV: Swinging on a Postmodern Star," in *Cultural Politics in Contemporary America*, ed. Ian Angus and Sut Jhally (NY: Routledge, 1989), p. 262.

36. Grossberg, "MTV," 261.

37. Stuart Ewen, "Advertisement and the Development of Consumer Society," in *Cultural Politics in Contemporary America*, p. 85.

38. Ewen, "Advertisement and the Development of Consumer Society," p. 95.

39. C. Wright Mills, "The Mass Society," in *Man Alone*, ed. Eric and Mary Josephson (NY: Dell, 1962), p. 217.

40. John Schwartz, "Stalking the Youth Market," in *Newsweek* (special edition: "The New Teens: What Makes Them Different?") (Summer/Fall, 1990), p. 36.

41. Michael Hirschorn, "Why MTV Matters," *Esquire* (October, 1990), p. 90.

42. Kaplan, "Feminism/Oedipus/Postmodernism," p. 36.

43. Kevin Kelley, "Selling the World: Mouseketeers to Marketeers," *Whole Earth Review* (Winter, 1989), p. 36.

44. Will Baker, "The Global Teenager," *Whole Earth Review* (Winter, 1989), p. 35.

45. Pepsi's foray into multiculturalism here owes a debt to a series of print ads for "the United Colors of Benetton." The Benetton ads depict a hip, multinational teen community brought together by their common interest in cotton clothing. Describing the "Benetton ideology" implicit in these ads, black filmmaker Isaac Julien aptly quips: "Erase your history, and we'll all be happy." See: James Saynor, "Young Soul Rebels," *Interview*, vol. 22, no. 1 (January, 1991), p. 24.

Chapter Five—The Apolitics of Style

1. Dick Hebdige citing "Punks Have Mothers Too: They Tell Us a Few Home Truths" and "Punks and Mothers" in *Subculture: The Meaning of Style* (London: Methuen, 1979), pp. 158–159.

2. Greil Marcus, *Lipstick Traces: A Secret History of the Twentieth Century* (Cambridge: MA: Harvard University Press, 1989), p. 70.

3. Marcus, *Lipstick Traces*, p. 205.

4. Hebdige, *Subculture: The Meaning of Style*, p. 25.

5. Hebdige, *Subculture*, p. 64.

6. Hebdige, *Subculture*, p. 115.

7. Marcus, *Lipstick Traces*, p. 38.

8. Marcus, *Lipstick Traces*, p. 17.

9. Andrew Herman, "You're Under Suspicion: Punk and the Secret History of the Twentieth Century," *Versions*, no. 1 (1990), p. 87.

10. Marcus, *Lipstick Traces*, p. 202.

11. John Clarke, "The Skinheads and the Magical Recovery of Working Class Community," in *Resistance Through Rituals*, ed. Stuart Hall, John Clarke, Tony Jefferson, and Brian Roberts (London: Hutchinson, 1976).

12. Hebdige, *Subculture: The Meaning of Style*, p. 79.

13. Gary Clarke, "Defending Ski-Jumpers: A Critique of Theories of Youth Subcultures," in *On Record: Rock, Pop and the Written Word*, ed. Simon Frith and Andrew Goodwin (NY: Pantheon, 1990), p. 86.

14. Angela McRobbie, "Settling Accounts With Subcultures: A Feminist Critique," p. 73.

15. Herman, "You're Under Suspicion," p. 88.

16. Edward Ball, "The Connoisseurship of Hype," *Afterimage*, vol. 16, no. 5 (December, 1988), p. 3.

17. Taylor as cited by Ball, "The Connoisseurship of Hype," p. 3.

18. Ball, "The Connoisseurship of Hype," p. 3.

19. McLaren as cited by Ball, "The Connoisseurship of Hype," p. 3.

20. The title of the symposium is an allusion to Guy Debord's *Society of the Spectacle* and an affirmation of McLaren's ties with the Situationist International.

21. McLaren as cited by Ball, "The Connoisseurship of Hype," p. 20.

22. Terrence Rafferty, "*Sid and Nancy,*" *The Nation* (November 1, 1988), p. 467.

23. Hebdige, *Subculture: The Meaning of Style*, pp. 121–123.

24. Maurizio Viano, "*Sid and Nancy*," *Film Quarterly* (Spring, 1987), p. 34.

25. Janet Bergstrom, "Androids and Androgeny," *Camera Obscura*, vol. 15 (Fall, 1986), p. 55.

26. Bergstrom, "Androids and Androgeny," p. 48.

27. J. Hoberman, "No Wavelength: The Para-Punk Underground," *Village Voice* (May 21, 1979), pp. 42–43.

28. Fred Pfeil, "Makin' Flippy-Floppy: Postmodernism and the Baby Boom PMC," in *The Year Left*, ed. Mike Davis, Michael Sprinker, and Fred Pfeil (London: Verso, 1985), p. 285.

29. An apt term coined by Dolores Hayden in "Capitalism, Socialism and the Built Environment," in *Socialist Visions*, ed. Steve Rosskam Shalom (Boston: South End, 1983), p. 60.

30. Pfeil, "Makin' Flippy-Floppy," p. 286.

31. "Creative Methodologies," *Wet* (May/June 1981), p. 61.

32. Theodor Adorno, "On Popular Music," in *On Record: Rock, Pop and the Written Word*, p. 308.

33. Adorno, "On Popular Music," p. 311.

34. Adorno, "On Popular Music," p. 313.

35. Adorno, "On Popular Music," p. 313.

36. Simon Frith, *Sound Effects: Youth, Leisure and the Politics of Rock 'n' Roll* (NY: Pantheon, 1981), p. 129.

37. Frith, *Sound Effects*, p. 201.

38. Lawrence Grossberg, "Is there Rock After Punk?," in *On Record: Rock, Pop and the Written Word*, p. 113.

39. Grossberg, "Is there Rock After Punk?," p. 116.

40. Bernard Gendron, "Theodor Adorno and the Cadillacs," in *Studies in Entertainment*, ed. Tania Modleski (Bloomington: Indiana University Press, 1986), p. 19.

41. Gendron, "Theodor Adorno," p. 34.

42. Gendron, "Theodor Adorno," p. 34.

Chapter Six—The Road to Ruin

1. Dana Polan, "Brief Encounters: Mass Culture and the Evacuation of Sense," in *Studies in Entertainment*, ed. Tania Modleski (Bloomington: Indiana University Press, 1986), p. 175.

2. Polan, "Brief Encounters," p. 182.

3. Polan, "Brief Encounters," p. 183.

4. Polan, "Brief Encounters," p. 182.

5. Fredric Jameson, "Postmodernism and Consumer Society," in *Postmodernism and Its Discontents*, ed. E. Ann Kaplan (NY: Verso, 1988), pp. 18–20. Jameson has the following to say about the contemporary nostalgia film: "We must conceive of this category in the broadest way: narrowly defined, no doubt, it consists merely of films about the past and about specific generational moments of that past." Contemporary nostalgia films like *American Graffiti, Chinatown, Star Wars* and *Body Heat,* Jameson argues, are not about a real, lived historical past. Instead, they reinvent "the feel and the shape of characteristic art objects of an older period." Nostalgia films these days, Jameson concludes, are defined by their net effect: they "trigger nostalgic reactions" and in doing so at once exist "beyond history" and graphically display "our" collective inability to "(achieve) aesthetic representations of our current experience."

6. Jameson, "Postmodernism," pp. 16, 18.

7. Jameson, "Postmodernism," p. 20.

8. Jameson, "Postmodernism," p. 18.

9. David Sheff, "George Lucas (interview)," *Rolling Stone* (December 10, 1987), p. 241.

10. Sheff, "George Lucas," p. 242.

11. Robert Hatch, "Films (a review of *American Graffiti*)," *The Nation* (September 24, 1973), p. 283. (The parenthetical digression is mine.)

12. Hatch, "Films," p. 283.

13. In *Hollywood from Vietnam to Reagan* (NY: Columbia University Press, 1986), Robin Wood makes a similar point by juxtaposing the sexist postscript of *American Graffiti* to the more egalitarian (but equally banal and unnecessary) postscript of *Fast Times at Ridgemont High* (p. 219).

14. The Hughes films are not alone in their nostalgic focus on class (im)mobility. See also *The Wanderers* (Philip Kaufman, 1979), *The Lords of Flatbush* (Stephen Verona/Martin Davidson, 1974), *The Outsiders* (Francis Coppola, 1983), *Dirty Dancing* (Emile Andolino, 1987), *Valley Girl* (Martha Coolidge, 1983), and *Cry-Baby* (John Waters, 1990).

15. Northrop Frye, *Anatomy of Criticism* (Princeton: Princeton University Press, 1957).

16. Jim Leach, "The Screwball Comedy," in *Film Genre: Theory and Criticism*, ed. Barry K. Grant (Metuchen, NJ: Scarecrow, 1977), p. 80. Here Leach is building on Robin Wood's notion of "the lure of the impossible." See Wood, *Howard Hawks* (London: Secker and Warburg, 1968), p. 78.

17. David R. Shumway, "Screwball Comedies: Constructing Romance, Mystifying Marriage," *Cinema Journal*, vol. 30, no. 4 (Summer, 1991), p. 7.

18. Geoff Pevere, "Rebel Without a Chance: Cycles of Rebellion and Suppression in Canadian Teen Movies," *CineAction*, no. 12 (April, 1988), pp. 45–46.

19. S.E. Hinton, *Rumble Fish* (NY: Dell, 1975), p. 30.

20. Hinton, *Rumble Fish*, p. 103.

21. The lyrics to a song performed by the Rhode Island bar-band "The Young Adults," aptly titled "It's A Complex World."

22. Andrew Kopkind "Movies (A review of *JFK*)," *Vogue* (January, 1991), p. 67.

23. Will Baker, "The Global Teenager," *Whole Earth Review* (Winter, 1989), p. 25.

24. Baker, "Global Teenager," p. 19.

25. *Youth in the Eighties* (Lausanne, Switzerland: Unesco Press, 1981), p. 17.

26. David Gelman, "A Much Riskier Passage," *Newsweek* (Special edition: "The New Teens: What Makes Them Different?"), p. 12.

Index

Index

heavy metal, 17–19, 79
Hebdige, Dick, 5–7, 10, 40, 41, 64, 67, 72, 77–78, 84–85, 100, 106–109, 115, 126
Heckerling, Amy, 72, 74
Hell, Richard, 112
Helter Skelter, 36–37
Hendrix, Jimi, 123
Hcnlcy, Don, 101
Herman, Andrew, 107, 109
High Noon, 29
High School, 45–46
Hills Have Eyes, The, 17
Hinton, S.E., 144
hippie(s), 16, 23, 36–39, 143
Hirsch, E.D. Jr., 53–54
Hirschi, Travis, 40
Hirschorn, Michael, 100
Hopper, Dennis, 14, 42, 100, 134
horror movies, 16–17, 66–69, 144
Howard, Ron, 134
Hughes, John, 138–141
Hunter, Tim, 14, 19
Huxley, Aldous, 137, 138

In-Between Love, 68–70

JFK, 150
Jackson, Michael, 101, 102
Jameson, Fredric, 129, 129n5, 131, 150
Jezer, Marty, 54
John, Elton, 102
Joplin, Janis, 123
Jones, Steve, 113
Josephson, Eric and Mary, 24

Kaplan, E. Ann, 98, 100–102
Karate Kid, The, 49
KC and the Sunshine Band, 84
Keniston, Kenneth, 5, 9–10, 15n10, 24, 34
Kennedy, John F., 133, 136, 150
Kern, Richard, 118
Kidnapped, 118
Kinsey, Alfred, 57–58, 61, 64, 66
Kinsey Report, the, 57, 61, 66
Kopkind, Andrew, 150
Kornhauser, William, 24

Kramer vs. Kramer, 26
Kruger, Freddy, 17
Kubrick, Stanley, 43

Ladies and Gentlemen The Fabulous Stains, 98
Last American Virgin, The, 72, 72n33
Last House on the Left, The, 17
Leach, Jim, 139
Lean On Me, 49–51, 52
Leary, Timothy, 37
Leave It to Beaver, 142
Lee, Spike, 101
Lefebvre, Henri, 109
LeMat, Paul, 134
Less Than Zero, 33
Lester, Richard, 88–89, 91
Levi-Strauss, Claude, 78, 109
Levin, Murray, 24
Leyton, Elliot, 18
Liquid Jesus, 13
Liquid Sky, 116–118
Live Aid, 123
Lord of the Flies, 23
Lords of Flatbush, The, 138n14
Love Me Tonight, 82
Lucas, George, 27, 133–137
Lunch, Lydia, 118
Lynch, David, 131

MacInnes, Colin, 79–82
Madonna, 98–99, 101
Mailer, Norman, 20, 41
Malick, Terrence, 32
Manhattan Love Suicides, 118
Manson, Charles, 16, 35–39
Marcus, Greil, 107–109
Masters, William H. and Johnson, Virginia E., 57–58, 64, 66
Maynard, Fredelle B., 47
McLaren, Malcom, 110–115, 119
McRobbie, Angela, 63–64, 70, 78, 109
Mead, Margaret, 59
Mellancamp, John Cougar, 102
melodrama, 13, 20–21, 47, 120, 144, 151n27
Merton, Robert K., 15–16
method, the, 20, 145

171

Index

OCT 16 1995

AUG 1 8 2005

D0728496

The Road to
Romance & Ruin